My Father! My Father!

SAM SOLEYN
WITH
NICHOLAS SOLEYN

Soleyn Publishing LLC
PO Box 67456, Albuquerque,
NM 87193-7456, USA
www.soleynpublishing.com
contact@soleynpublishing.com
facebook.com/soleynpublishing
twitter.com/SoleynPublish

Generation Culture Transformation
Specializing in publishing for generation culture change

eGenCo. LLC
824 Tallow Hill Road
Chambersburg, PA- 17202, USA
Phone: 717-461-3436
email: info@egenco.com
Website: www.egenco.com
          www.egenbooks.com

facebook.com/egenbooks
twitter.com/vishaljets
youtube.com/egenpub
egenco.com/blog

Paperback ISBN 978-1-936554-10-2
eBook ISBN 978-1-936554-11-9

For Worldwide Distribution, Printed in the U.S.A.

1 2 3 4 5 6 7 / 15 14 13 12 11

Many of the principles contained in this book were first experienced in practical reality within the context of my thirty-five year marriage to my beloved Lucy. The fruit of this marriage is two children, Tamarind and Nicholas. I was first introduced to the principles of fathering through my children. Tamarind is fond of saying that she taught me everything I know about fathering. It is with pleasure that I dedicate this book to Lucy and to Tamarind and Nicholas.

Acknowledgments

Among those who have influenced my thinking are legendary figures of literature such as John Milton, John Donne, Christopher Marlowe, Desiderius Erasmus, Dante Alighieri, Leo Tolstoy, and Thomas Hobbes. I have also been inspired by the insights of C.S. Lewis, Watchman Nee, and my friend and fellow laborer in the Kingdom, Thamo Naidoo. I have had discussions well into the night with Douglas Allen, Michael Barrett, and Corbett Gauldon, involving particular aspects of this book. To them and to a host of others who have contributed thoughts and insights, I am profoundly grateful. My principle acknowledgement, however, is to the Holy Spirit, the Spirit of Truth, who, under the direction of the Lord Jesus Christ, has pulled back the curtain and revealed mysteries that have been veiled in the folds of Scripture, waiting for a time and a generation for whom they were meant to be given as bread from heaven for this journey.

Foreword

The Church, by divine design, is patently and functionally the family or household of God. God created the human race to be the exact representatives of deity (Father, Son, Spirit) over all creation. The connection was that of the heavenly Father lovingly relating to a corporate Son on the earth, visibly expressing the glory of God.

On the practical side, when people receive Jesus Christ as their savior, they are placed into spiritual families whereby they are nurtured into the image of the Son of God (Psalm 68:6). In this way, God himself representatively fathers the fatherless and cares for the widow (James 1:27). Through this process, believers are resocialized and distinctly set apart from the families and organizations of the earth. If the church is God's family, then it should function as a family functions.

Herein lies the crux of the present problems confronting the Church. While the notion that the Church is the family of God is generally accepted by most denominational traditions of Christendom, its practical outworking is largely foreign. Overall, the Church has strayed from God's divine intention to have a family on the earth, and instead has fossilized into an institution of religion, encumbered by a plethora of regulations and practices. Consequently, since the family of God has abdicated its fundamental purpose, the earth is plagued with a curse, which can only be broken by fresh inquiry into the Scriptures concerning the Church's essential structure and apostolic mission. Not only will such inquiry reveal the predetermined plan of God in creating humankind, but it will also redress the question of the arrangement and management of God's household, and reveal the need for the restoration of "father leaders" who will selflessly raise up the sons of God to steward the Kingdom of God (Malachi 4:6), thereby establishing the sovereign rule of peace in creation.

It is against this backdrop that *My Father! My Father!* by Sam Soleyn is timely, clinically diagnosing the present problems in Church and society. He addresses the identity, purpose, and function of the Church of Jesus Christ, and maintains that a crisis of identity produces a malfunction in behavior—the cause of the gross darkness that is covering the earth. The cure, according to Sam, is the necessity for a restructuring of God's family. Fundamentally, he is challenging the ecclesiology of the 21st Century Church. This does not imply the proposal of a new biblical order. By Sam's own admission, the views in his book are not new, being first revealed in early antiquity. His hypothesis is supported by Old Covenant patterns, typifying and pointing to the manner in which the New Covenant people are constituted. He is simply imploring the Church to return to the original divine arrangement.

While records of these truths are not new to those schooled in the history of Christianity, they are a breath of fresh air to any who desire change. Sam's insights are revelatory in that they emerge at a time when a new hour has dawned upon the Church—a time for the reformation of thought and praxis.

Undoubtedly, this book is groundbreaking in that it resets the boundaries of our habitation by advocating a more excellent way in which believers may function as the sons of God in the earth. This is a paradigmatic shift from many traditional and more recent philosophical and humanistic ideals prevalent in church circles. This book is a witness against prevailing pagan systems of Christianity, which enslave the children of God and prevent them from enjoying the liberty made available through Jesus Christ. It's a clarion call for the restoration and reconstitution of the predetermined divine intent; the realization of a corporate son in the image of Christ—the firstborn Son (Romans 8:29).

To reach this objective, Sam posits that the theocracy of the Church is fundamentally patriarchal in nature—the family of God is managed by fathers (elders). These individuals function representatively as servants, custodians, and guardians of the divine heirs to the covenant (Galatians 4:1). Fathers graciously and lovingly shepherd the flock of God with "bread from heaven" (Exodus 16:4). Under the executive leadership of the Holy Spirit, they guide the sons of God through the wilderness of life into maturity, so that the divine family may realize their calling and ministry in this world. The objective is the strategic placement of mature sons into influential places in the world so that the kingdoms of the earth may be brought under the rule of Christ.

On a personal note, I reflect on my relationship with Sam Soleyn. In life there are those rare encounters that indelibly mark our journey. Often unexpected, these moments fine-tune our perspectives and order our steps in Christ. These are divine appointments, opening vistas of new spiritual experience. Such was my meeting with Sam.

I met Sam at The Apostolic Declaration Conference, hosted by Eugene and Patrice Sheppard in Washington, DC, 2005. My first impression of Sam was that of a true statesman of noble character, exuding the wisdom of the ages. This was a servant and apostle of Christ who not only commanded the presence of God, but also accurately communicated the culture of the Kingdom with grace and ease. His persona typified what it is to be a son and father in the household of God. Not only did my spirit jump at the sound of his voice and the clarity of his understanding of the times we are living in, but it also responded to the call for covenantal relationship that Sam and I have today, for which I am eternally grateful.

As the seed of our relationship blossomed, we would deliberate over the Word of God and His kingdom into the early parts of the morning. To me, these were priceless opportunities for being sharpened and polished. During these engagements, I discovered the depth of the man. A reservoir of knowledge, bringing the gift of wisdom to bear upon our conversations, he was also practical in the manner in which he translated his knowledge to life and, more specifically, to people. It was clear early in our relationship that he did not only carry a divine message, but that he had become the message. Having observed his relationships with others, it was clear that his leadership ability was that of a father intimately relating to his children. His whole disposition embodied the patriarchal grace of the Father.

Finally, in my estimate, Sam's views on God's family are not simply philosophical; he has imparted his whole life. His relationships with a host of dynamic people across the earth underpin this reality. Simply stated, he is a patriarch in the Kingdom of God who has raised many sons, some to the place of fathering multiple households in the Church and in corporate society. In this respect, the authenticity of *My Father! My Father!* is not merely the communication of a profound revelation, but of the heavenly grace incarnate in the life of the writer who has become the revelation. This book will undoubtedly contribute to the restoration of the Church to its glorious prophetic and consummate destiny in Christ.

Thamo Naidoo
River of Life Christian Ministries
Pietermaritzburg, South Africa

reface

I believe it is important to read *My Father! My Father!* within context. Therefore, I offer this brief revelation of my background. I was born on the island of Saint Vincent in the Caribbean and am a person of mixed race, with predominant strains being Indian, African, Portuguese, and English. Under the British system, I received a classical education until I left the islands at the age of eighteen for further studies in the United States. In college I studied rhetoric, law, and theology, gaining undergraduate degrees in English and Speech and a juris doctorate from the University of New Mexico School of Law in 1982.

My beginnings as a preacher include a background with the Anglican Church, which forms part of my exposure to the historic church. I now work extensively among widely diverse nations— from the United States to countries in Africa, Europe, the Caribbean, and the former Soviet Union—and among even more widely diverse racial groups.

I preached my first message in my fifteenth year of life, and now have spent forty-five years in and around church circles that are as varied as the cultures that produce them. I was a believer for nearly twenty years before the reality of God, separate and apart from religion, became clear to me. Before that time, successful interpretation of Scripture blended the influences of societal culture and religious practices in which the normal paradigm for my interpretation of Scripture was historic traditions of interpretation mixed with the preference of societal appeal. In my wide-ranging field of experience over the decades, however, I became aware of the fact that the culture of religion mitigates against the knowledge of God.

I was introduced to the reality of the person of God in a Damascus-Road-style experience in 1984. Experiencing the person of God Himself opened the eyes of my spirit to a reality that greatly transcended religious normalcy. It opened my spirit to the reality of the realm of the Spirit. I was instantly transformed, internally, and from that time, I have been exploring the invisible reality of God, the Kingdom of Heaven, and the realm of the Spirit.

Recognizing my own transformation, great care has been taken to note the biblical references relevant to the assertions made within the text. We fully anticipate that the revelations in this book will challenge, and even overthrow, closely held beliefs and long-standing religious traditions.

Given much of the focus on the relationship between fathers and sons in this book, there is no irony that my faithful co-laborer in this and in future planned projects is my son, Nicholas Soleyn. He has participated extensively in the underlying research, writing, and editing of this book, and under my direction is already heavily involved in the planning of future works. We have discussed fully all of the chapters, their content and arrangements, and he is quite familiar with the subject matter and my thought processes. He is properly listed with me as one of the authors of this book. I am indebted to him for his invaluable participation and contributions.

In committing these revelations to writing, I have been fully helped on the journey by the blessed Holy Spirit whom Jesus sent upon His return to heaven to reveal Himself to humans and to restore the knowledge of God and His intentions for the creation of man. For the most part, the revelations contained herein are not new revelations, but are the illumination of revelations already written within the Old and New Testaments. According to Scripture, some revelations are rolled up and sealed "till the time of the end," (Daniel 12:9 KJV) and then they are revealed to the generation for whom they are meant. I believe the revelations contained in this book are for this time on the earth.

There are many necessary and fundamental questions asked by those who are earnestly seeking God. To them, the answers found in religious traditions have proven inadequate or completely absent. This book establishes a framework in which to think about these questions and begin to answer them in accordance with Scripture and the Holy Spirit.

This work is deliberately limited to establishing the principles of the relationship between God and man. It is an overarching picture that presents a contrast to the traditional religious mindset and, as such, offers very different answers, but it does not advance into practical applications. It is a foundation upon which we will build.

Sam Soleyn

My Father! My Father!

Introduction

I will not leave you as orphans; I will come to you.[1]

Before God created the world, He covenanted with Himself to establish the purpose and order of humankind in creation. The world would be the venue in which the covenant would be fulfilled, and man the principle actor in the drama of its unfolding. God knew the end of the story from the beginning.

His purposes for creating the world were to put on display His nature of love and to expunge the taint of sin from creation. God created a son, Adam, to whom He gave the mandate to rule. He arranged the order of creation to facilitate His son's rule and invested His son with the authority to represent the culture of heaven in the earth.

The enemy, who rebelled against God's choice of man as His heirs, introduced sin into creation through Adam. Inevitably, both Adam and Christ, the sons sent from heaven to display the nature of the love of God, were destined to confront the enemy. In Adam's unsuccessful confrontation, separation from God and the attendant fatherless culture resulted.

When man separated himself from his Father, his culture changed from that of a son to the culture of an orphan, which became the de facto human culture. The culture of a son differs entirely from that of an orphan. A son of God in creation is designated to radiate the glory of God's nature and to represent exactly the nature of his Father by ruling in the spheres of his authority as the Father would. He is supported in these twin imperatives by the resources of his Father's house; whereas an orphan relies exclusively upon himself for his provision and protection, and his goal is to survive. The fall of man introduced this culture as an alternative to the original intention of God for the creation of man.

In the precreation covenant, God provided for the redemption of His house. "[T]he Lamb [was] slain from the foundation of the world" so that the mandates associated with God's son in the earth would proceed to their final manifestations.[2] At the appropriate time, therefore, God sent another son to redeem His house and to reestablish His purposes for His sons. Jesus appeared at the appointed time to redeem man from the results of Adam's choice.

Christ successfully confronted the enemy and succeeded in overthrowing all of the consequences of his deception. Jesus lived upon the earth in a manner distinct from all other humans. He showed man that it is possible to hear God and to walk in divine order moment by moment. His declaration, that "[m]an shall not live on bread alone, but on every word that comes from the mouth of God," was meant to explain how He lived and who He was, because He also was the Bread from heaven and the Word that proceeded from the mouth of God.[3] His life was a complete display of the life God originally intended His sons to live upon the earth. He has made available, to all humanity, the opportunity to be reconciled to God the Father and to put on display God's glory, His love.

God raised Jesus from the dead as "both Lord and Christ." Christ is a reference to the corporate anointing to which all the sons of God, born again of the Spirit, are assembled as His body. Jesus himself ascended to heaven and now sits on the throne of God as the head.

Jesus' accomplishment in overthrowing the enemy's deception

has resulted in the reintroduction of the authority of heaven as the alternative basis of power and rule, supporting the activities of the sons of God upon the earth. This basis of authority is known as the Kingdom of God. The Kingdom of God is a functioning reality upon the earth that gives order and form to the children of God as they pursue the purposes of God, collectively, as the Body of Christ.

THE HOUSE OF GOD

The family of God on the earth is a spiritual family, drawn from all the ranks of humanity and formed into an arrangement that presents the fundamental nature of God's love. The sons of God who make up this family are spirit beings, since God Himself is a spirit. Although in their relationships with each other sons of God may be male and female, from different races, from various ethnic backgrounds, and from different social classes, in their relationship to God the Father, they are all sons. The entire House of God is arranged to show the love of a father for a son and the trust of a father by a son. This central value is presented with greater complexity through the order of a spiritual family, household, clan, tribe, and eventually a nation.

The spiritual body, comprising all the sons of God, exists simultaneously in heaven and on earth, and it is the House of God in both realms. The order of its arrangement is designed to display the culture of heaven on the earth. The foundation of this culture is the order of father and son through which the love of God is presented on the earth as it is in heaven.

For nearly two millennia, religious thought has focused upon gaining access to heaven in the afterlife and has offered no explanation for God's placement of man upon the earth. All the narratives begin with the story in progress, starting with the Garden of Eden. At that starting point, the focus comes to be on the need for the redemption of man. No consideration is given to the prior question of why God created man as His son and put him to rule on the earth.

This book tells the story of God's original intention for the creation of man and explains how the sacrifice of Jesus on the cross repositions man in the will of God so that he is able to fulfill God's intention for creating him.

CHAPTER 1

The Fatherless Culture

Culture is the foundation of our identity, individually and as members of society. It is the memory, speech, art, and behavior passed from one generation to the next. An individual interprets his or her unique experiences predictably, in a manner consistent with cultural norms, which in turn forms the basis for self-perception. Culture dictates how each person defines his or her self. The legacy of society's forebears lies in the characteristics of its cultural identity. That identity can be so ingrained within an individual that, without the revelation of a different culture, it defines the course of his life. Whether or not he is aware of this fact is irrelevant to the outcome.

Today, the dominant global culture is that of fatherlessness. This culture is a subtle and pervasive one that teaches people to think like orphans. It is a culture separated from the beneficial influence of one's forebears and leaves the orphan defenseless in his own mind. An orphan has no protection and no provision other than what he can create for himself and must struggle for survival by whatever means necessary.

Today's fatherless culture directly conflicts with the culture of the Kingdom of God. Whereas a fatherless culture produces orphans, God created man to be His children and heirs to His

Kingdom. The culture of the Kingdom of God is that of a house. The conflict between these two cultures has come to a head as God continues to reveal his House on the earth.

The House of God is the family of God. It exists simultaneously in heaven and on earth.[4] The Kingdom of God is the base of authority and rule that empowers His House in both domains. The Kingdom exists to support the children of God in their mandate to represent the nature and character of God Himself. It is designed to restore the original intent of God for the creation of man and, in the process, to rescue humankind from the culture of the orphan. The House of God is being revealed at this time to provide God's children with the righteous alternative to the earth's pervasive fatherless culture.

THE NEW GLOBAL CULTURE

The inheritance to which a child is entitled from a father is the love, support, and resources of a household. At a minimum, this requires a meaningful relationship between the father and his children. Applying this minimal standard highlights the pandemic scope of the problem; the predominant global culture is that of orphans. This culture so completely permeates nations, people groups, and religions that fatherlessness has become the standard against which all other cultural profiles are, consciously or unconsciously, compared. Therefore, the concept of continuity through inheritance is foreign to most of the world's societies.

The modern orphan comes in many forms. Changing social patterns, war and disease, politics, and the failings of religious systems in the many corners of the world have created orphans out of entire nations and entire generations of people. Where these phenomena have removed the father from the average family unit, children are left to figure out how to survive on their own, and eventually they impart their identity as orphans to their children.

The traditional family structure has changed in ways that deprive children of a minimal relationship with their father, even when the father is alive or physically present. Until recently, having children born out of wedlock or into a relationship of unmarried co-habitation was stigmatizing in Western societies. Today, however, one of the largest contributions to the absence of fathers in Western culture is the number of children being born to single mothers. In the United States, approximately 41 percent of new births are to unmarried women.[5] Similar rates of birth outside of marriage occur in England and other European countries.[6]

Fatherlessness in the United States is not centered on a particular demographic. That more than half of all children in the African-American community are living in fatherless homes is particularly striking. However, over 42 percent of white marriages end in divorce.[7] Whereas African-American children are being born into fatherless homes, white children are increasingly made fatherless through divorce.

While changes in social norms contribute to a more subtle development of a fatherless culture, war and disease have made orphans of entire nations almost overnight. In Central and Southern Africa, the AIDS epidemic has removed an entire generation of fathers and has reshaped the social structure. When parents are lost to disease, children become the heads of households with the responsibility to raise and care for their younger siblings. They are orphans raising orphans.

Similarly, the fruit of war yields an abundant crop of orphans. For example, in countries that made up the former Federal Republic of Yugoslavia, civil wars have destroyed the social structure and debased the role of fathers among the people. Many families were destroyed by violence, and mass campaigns that used rape as a weapon of war and "ethnic cleansing" resulted in the births of thousands of orphans, most of whose current status is unknown.[8] Such a sizable population of orphans begot of violence robs an entire generation of its identity. Moreover, the aftermath of war and revolution has left the door open for human traffickers, whose prey is the vulnerable children of these countries. Countries that were part of the former Yugoslavia are now key staging areas for "recruiting" children for the massive Eastern European sex trade.

3

The children of these nations have been left open to attack and exploitation. They have no basis for understanding the love and protection of a father.

Communism's Role

In the wake of communism are millions of orphans and a family infrastructure that has not recovered its identity, since being defined solely as part of the state's resources. Under communist rule, the state had the final authority over children, and parental control was subject to state interests. Families were units of the state, and the state controlled the children's destinies. Communism stripped nations of a working model of family life, and these newly independent nations have no foundation on which to build a social infrastructure.

Social phenomena in former communist countries demonstrate plainly the effect communism has had on the family unit. As an example, in the Ukraine, one of the most popular television programs is a program on family relationships, hosted by an evangelical preacher turned politician. He saw that the nation's chances of survival were very slim without the reintroduction of this essential building block, the family, to the nation. The vast number of orphans, relative to the overall population, places the future of the nation at risk.

The national churches in these former communist countries are marked by their cooperative relationship with the toppled regimes. The churches offer little more than liturgical practices that are generally outdated and out of touch with the people. As a result, there is no significant spiritual alternative to the godless legacies of atheistic communism. This pattern replays itself from Russia to Cuba and involves entire nations and almost all of their populations.

The fatherless culture represents the largest demographic grouping of humanity today and has invaded every aspect of human society. The systems of the world are feeding this culture, and in its inexorable rise, the culture of the fatherless is redefining social norms globally. Because of its pervasiveness, this culture is virtually unnoticed. Sociologists, demographers, politicians, and marketers all study different manifestations of this culture as it relates to those particular areas of interests. However, few have seen the fatherless culture as the overarching influence, which has infused itself into every aspect of life. Viewed with an understanding of the culture of the fatherless, the trends throughout the world and in all areas of society illustrate that the fatherless culture currently defines human society.

RELIGION AS A CAUSE OF FATHERLESSNESS

Rather than offering an alternative to fatherlessness, churches have been shaped by this prevailing culture and, in their malleability, failed to impart the wisdom and revelation of the Kingdom of God to the culture of orphans. Where confronted with a fatherless culture, religious systems have been revealed as the byproducts of spurious traditions.

Religions with patriarchal forms tend to subsist on formulaic rules taken from outdated interpretations of sacred writings—usually a blend of history, customs, and traditions. Their antiquated practices do not foster a connection with the people. As such, these religions resort to shame-based manipulation and appeal to the fear of being stigmatized in the community to control its members' conduct. That these religions advance their ideologies through manipulation and intimidation is a clear sign the spirit of a loving father is absent from within them.

The only goals religion can offer are those that feed the desires of their sponsorship. Where the predominant culture is one of fatherlessness, the religious systems bend to cater to the desires of the orphaned society. They offer the possibility of financial success or victory over one's personal or social oppressors as the great objective for surviving our time on this earth. Love is not a requirement. Nothing in these models suggests that the god of the religion loves you, nor are you required to love the god. Instead, they teach that strict adherence to orthodoxy will lead to the fulfillment of these basic desires.

What happens when a nation of orphans is offered only anachronistic practices that carry the fear of punishment and the threat of exclusion? In the family dynamic, the father models the attitude of the god at the center of the religious faith. If the goal is conformity, and fathers are the enforcers, then the belief system itself is valued more than the well-being of a child. A father's love is both constrained by, and subservient to, the religious requirements. One of the most horrendous examples of this phenomenon is the practice of honor killings: putting a child to death for infractions—either willful or unknowing—against the orthodoxy. Killing a child to preserve one's honor in the name of any religious tradition empties that patriarchal religious order of the righteous concept of fathering.

Embodying fatherlessness in religion are those priests who have violated the persons of their most vulnerable charges. These religious figures, which have purloined the title of "fathers," have committed unconscionable and criminal acts against children, haplessly left in their charge. In protecting these miscreants for fear of legal liabilities, the church hierarchy has abandoned the people in favor of protecting its patriarchal order. The church has reinforced the orphan mentality and bolstered the fatherless culture.

These religious systems disseminate a false vision of God the Father to a fatherless culture. The vision of a loving father has been lost to the imperative of preserving the institution. The rituals remain intact, and the words say, "God is love." Yet the practices of the religious orders have denied any truth contained in either the words or the rituals. By widening the gap between people and God, the religious system's contribution to the culture of fatherlessness is incalculably harmful.

THE MANY FORMS OF FATHERLESSNESS

The development of a culture depends upon the society's means and capacity for passing knowledge to successive generations. The most common manner of passing along cultural knowl-

6

edge is through interactions with one another. Therefore, one can observe the characteristics of a culture in the relationships between the people that model the cultural patterns.

The culture of the fatherless is most readily evident in the attitude of fathers toward their children. Fathers will model the image of a father that is presented to them, either by their own parents, media depictions of fathers, or their peers. Where the standard in the culture is an absent father, the culture raises up fathers who are abusive or uninterested in their families.

The following anecdotal story highlights the pervasive character of the fatherless culture.

> *I once received a call from a woman concerned about her husband, a former successful business executive, who had abruptly adopted self-destructive behavior. She explained that her husband had recently taken an early retirement, and shortly after, he became withdrawn and isolated to the severe degeneration of his physical and mental health, his family's relationship and finances, and his role as a father.*
>
> *Retiring early, the husband had planned to spend his extra time pursuing a different life from his business activities. He expressed an interest in travel, and after that, he wanted to pursue an interest in painting. Within a few months, however, these pursuits became lost in a fog of disinterest. He brooded, communicated in short, terse sentences, and showed little interest in his family's activities and well-being. Their efforts to motivate him were rebuffed, and he retreated into silence. His family began to observe the growing signs of depression, and his physical health began to reflect his mental health. His days were spent watching television and eating junk food, while his wife was left to manage the family's affairs, without income or support.*
>
> *I asked the husband to explain what he thought were the problems. At first, he did not acknowledge there was a problem, but then he offered a superficial analysis. He suggested that it*

was not too unusual to have a period of transition character-ized by rest and inactivity following a busy career. He further suggested that his wife was unused to having him home and was unnecessarily concerned about his lack of motivation.

The wife had a very different view. She and the rest of the family agreed that the husband had changed dramatically in the months following his retirement. She was particularly concerned about their college-aged son who seemed most af-fected and was beginning to express his anger and frustration by small acts of uncharacteristic rebellion.

I then asked the husband to comment on his relationship with his father. He was slow to respond and became notice-ably uncomfortable. After some urging, the husband told me that his father had died when he was still quite young, and his mother had raised him, as a single parent.

His memories of his father were mostly of painful events. The most vivid of which was how he had been pun-ished when, at three years old, his father caught him playing with matches. His father's discipline was to hold his hand to a lighted match until his fingers blistered, ignoring the boy's screams and his mother's pleas to stop. In the man's memory, the pain of rejection was as fresh as if it had only recently occurred, and as he told me the story, he was in the emotional state of that small boy again. Each of the memories that he related highlighted his pain of rejection by his father.

Curiously, he offered the explanation that his father was just trying to show his love, even in these harsh acts of disci-pline. He justified his father's behavior by suggesting that it was the only way his father understood to do what he deemed necessary, since, having been similarly abandoned, he had no training from his own father.

The husband further told me that he had never seen himself as a happy person. He had started working and contributing to his family's finances at a young age; and since then, he mea-sured his value by his ability to work hard and to provide well.

He added that there were moments of happiness throughout his life, such as his wedding and the birth of his children, but he had always felt alone and that he kept people at a distance all of his life. He suggested that perhaps he was incapable of letting anyone into his true emotions. He concluded that, although he had not always been depressed, he always lived in anticipation of things going wrong or falling apart.

It became altogether apparent that I was observing, first-hand, the fatherless culture matured through at least three generations. The legacy of fatherlessness was his inheritance, and after at least three generations, it was the bedrock of his culture. Fatherlessness had become the paradigm by which he understood his own role as a father. This culture so completely identified him that, though he had tried hard to give his family a stable life, his children would too become fatherless, unless he somehow was able to change.

For a time, while he was pursuing his education and building his career, he was distracted from these cultural incidences. However, now that he was retired, this culture immediately reasserted itself and became the underlying cause of his depression. Once this was discovered, part of the solution was his obvious need for a spiritual father. Someone who could help him transition to an entirely different cultural experience and reverse the effects of his inherited culture.

An abusive or uninterested father alienates his children. Often, the result is anger toward the father and depression. Abuse may be either violent or nonviolent, and nonviolent abuse may be as effective as physical abuse in alienating a child. Harsh and humiliating words can destroy children's views of themselves and result in a profound sense of rejection. A silent or uninvolved father communicates to the child that the child's interests are of no particular value to the father, and therefore the child is unimportant.

Children raised in such environments do not feel that what they do is important, and they often feel that their existence is of no value. Such children do not normally think of having a destiny, but instead struggle every day with simply surviving. They grow up without clear models of behavior and are therefore more susceptible to outside pressures and temptations. They often adopt identities that are compatible with the instinct to survive.

THE VIEW OF FATHERS IN THE MEDIA

The pervasive nature of the fatherless culture is further exemplified in the popular culture's presentation of fathers. Media outlets act as a reference point for a culture and provide a window into the characteristics of a society. Because it represents the mainstream ideals and perspectives, the media both derives from and influences prevailing norms by catering to trends that are popular, intriguing, or entertaining. In various forms of reality and hyperbole, the media puts on display the culture of the society. If one is looking for evidence of a fatherless culture, that person need look no further.

The ideal man, the hero, typically is not a father, when portrayed in popular media. Most commonly, heroes are violent pillars of stoic masculinity. Not even Hollywood can place this kind of man into a family setting. Nonetheless, these archetypal heroes provide the model for young men who will one day be fathers. To reconcile the heroic ideal with the real-life role of the father requires lowering the bar for fatherhood. As a result, young men mimicking the cultural ideal of a hero will often abandon their own children with impunity.

When the entertainment industry takes the action hero and sufficiently waters him down to put him in a family setting, the resulting standard for fatherhood is bleak. Sitcoms seem to be the most common popular media in which men are presented in fatherly roles. The successful family sitcom typically portrays a bumbling husband and father who is consumed by self-interest and is distracted from the reality of family life around him. When his disconnectedness causes problems, the task falls to the mother or children to provide both obvious and insightful solutions. This formula spans the scope of television culture.

In the genre of reality television, popular culture shamelessly flaunts the base values of a fatherless culture. Few people object to the glorification of individuals who exhibit shocking displays of selfishness and disloyalty. Reality television has elevated some of the basest members of society to the status of cultural icons. As the society has taken a voyeuristic interest in its most grotesque qualities, this type of programming has exploded in popularity in recent years.

The depiction of fathers in the visual media is consistent with the overall decline in respect for fathers within the culture. With the type of societal changes evinced by rising divorce rates and the vast numbers of children born to single mothers, society is understandably apathetic to the portrayal of fathers in these ways. Changing the media, however, will not change the culture. The culture of the fatherless is ingrained in the society and only reflected in the media.

THE SPECTER OF AN ORPHAN CULTURE

The culture of the fatherless has fully invaded human society. Worldwide it takes many different forms, and it is reshaping global culture in fundamental ways. Survival and a search for an identity are goals of the orphan mindset produced by this culture. At its apex, the fatherless culture has usurped the individual's identity and replaced it with an identity dominated by a struggle for provision and protection.

In the Kingdom of God, each person's destiny is the playing out of that person's unique identity as a son of God, regardless of gender, race, or background. The culture of the Kingdom is a culture of kings, founded upon and modeled after God, the loving Father. This kingly culture cannot coexist with the fatherless culture. To embrace one's identity as a son, one must change his prevailing culture.

In this season, God is building His House in the earth, with the relationship of fathers and sons as its foundation. Effecting cultural change requires a trans-generational effort, in which a change in the culture is but one of the first steps of a long journey to reestablish, fully, the House of God. This journey is meant to reposition man in the relationship with God as Father, as God intended from the beginning. The purpose of repositioning humankind as sons and heirs to God is to establish the family of God on the earth and to display the love of God, through his sons, to all of creation. Whereas the destiny of each son of God is vitally important, the entire purpose of God can only, ultimately, be accomplished through the corporate form—the House of God.

CHAPTER 2

The Effects of the Fatherless Culture

This fatherless generation exists globally and has been imprinted with the identity of orphans. The worldwide spectrum of human activities, such as commerce, politics, and religion, are marked by the imperatives of this generation. It is reshaping these global systems in ways that are genuinely new and distinct. This has resulted in noticeable clashes with the settled cultural norms of previous generations, causing a rift between the fatherless generation and the older, more traditional, generations.

The reconciliation of the generations is an obvious imperative. Yet there appears to be no clear way forward. The competition between the generations has reached the point where there is a noticeable disconnect between the older generations and the fatherless generation. Entire communities lament this phenomenon, and in some segments of society the divide is seen as threatening the harmony and peace of the society itself.

A Generational Divide

The fatherless generation holds a deep-seated distrust of their fathers' generation. When the authority figures of their fathers' generation have attempted to influence the fatherless generation's direction, the younger generation has responded with contempt.

One illustration of the struggle over the widening gap between these generations is the efforts of Black civil rights leaders to address the images and lyrics associated with hip-hop music. For the past two decades, prominent leaders in the African-American community have criticized the lyrics of popular hip-hop music for its glorification of violence and its presentation of sexually explicit themes, particularly where those themes are seen as degrading toward women. They also have criticized the lifestyle associated with the hip-hop culture, which encourages a general disregard for authority and advocates conspicuous consumption, and they have descried the violence that has surrounded some of the leading figures within that culture, which has resulted in the incarceration and the untimely deaths of several of its luminaries. These leaders from the previous generations who have called for reform of this culture have been largely ignored by the fatherless generation.

The disconnect between the older authority figures and the fatherless generation is rooted largely in the younger generation's refusal to accept guidance from a generation from whom they feel estranged. The example of the clash over hip-hop culture and its results are foreseeable, because it represents a deep division within the African-American community, which has become largely a fatherless culture. Similar divisions occur across the spectrum of the interactions between the generations within the community. The culture of the orphan has confronted fathers from a previous generation, and the separation between the generations is a widening chasm.

POLITICAL DIVISIONS

An entire generation, regardless of demographics, exhibits the same fatherless characteristics. Current American politics provide a more general example of this growing divide between the generations. The younger generation has tended to support, en masse, the current president, who himself is fatherless. At the same time, it does not identify, in any general way, with the moral, ethical, and religious views of a more conservative constituency, since these views tend to represent the traditional perspectives of previous generations.

Internationally, this divide takes on different characteristics. Young Western-Europeans have gone on angry rampages, in countries such as France and England, to protest governmental decisions, ranging from employment legislation to college tuition hikes. They regard the use of political power as being opposed to their interests and see themselves permanently installed in states of poverty.

The problem of the division of generations takes on a different face in current and former communist nations. During the communist epoch, the state replaced the father as the dominant order of society. With the dissolution of the central authority of government, these nations have no practice with family-based authority. As a result, an abundant crop of orphans has sprung up throughout these former communist countries. This generation of orphans is merely biding their time to affect national changes according to their imperatives. For example, the central government of China has played the role of parents, to the denial of individual liberties and individual creativity, causing a growing frustration among the younger generation. This generation is now anticipating upcoming changes in the leadership of the central committee, which are expected to result in the voice of the next generation being heard for the first time at the highest levels of national government.

In the communist nations of Cuba and North Korea, the cults of personalities prevail. By contrast to the emerging former communist nations, the hope for change held by the younger generation in these countries is checked by the denial of access to the outside world through official government policy, enforced by the muscle of police power. In Cuba, the struggle for daily survival has eviscerated the family structure and created an entire nation of orphans.

Religion and caste systems have similarly divided societies in the Middle East and India, alienating generations of these vast populations. Rifts have appeared where the older generations cling to the power structures of tradition and the wealth and privilege of these structures, while these same structures have radicalized the younger generations. Internal civil conflicts challenge nations from Saudi Arabia to Pakistan, and the economic might of India is likely to run aground on the shoals of the vast underutilization of the populations confined to the disfavored castes.

CHARACTERISTICS OF THE FATHERLESS GENERATION

The fatherless generation considers the position of their fathers as being devoid of influence and relevance, and the older generation has largely concluded that the fatherless generation is self-centered and narcissistic. These positions are not the result of serious examinations of the rift between the two groups. The older generation is not considering the direction and consequences of the future that is being mapped out by the fatherless generation's prevailing influence. The younger generation is discounting what value might be derived from a more insightful evaluation of the history and culture of the fathers; and in the process, it runs the risk of substituting information for wisdom.

The center of this culture is an individualism that is beholden to a unique set of imperatives. The primary imperative is the need for an identity. Unconnected to an identity linked to past generations, the orphan must discover another basis for his identity. An identity that is connected to the past is one that potentially contains elements of one's forebears and of an inheritance. When this inheritance is empowering and enabling, it is like a springboard for a substantial leap forward for one's life. However, when the inheritance is a negative or hurtful legacy, it is a liability. The harsh truth is that for the majority of the fatherless generation, their image of a father is unpleasant and may be destructive to their sense of well-being, so they discard the past as a matter of survival. They remain fatherless by the choice to reject the pain of their experience and are obligated to forge an identity without reference to the past.

As a result, the individual is defined within the context of himself, and is responsible for his own provision and protection. The orphan does not expect to receive any measure of help from the generation of his father. Since he has inherited nothing of value from the past, he does not believe that a necessary part of his identity is to convey an inheritance to future generations. The resulting context of one's identity is the scope of a single lifetime, focused on present goals and circumstances. The orphan must define himself and his destiny in terms of what is attainable within the span of his own life. In this instant culture, he lives without reference to either the past or the future. He is himself fatherless and, therefore, naturally rejects the role of fathering. These are the essential characteristics of the need for provision and protection, and they permeate all areas in which the fatherless generation has significant influence.

The fatherless generation has access to nearly unlimited amounts of information. This generation makes connections globally and is not necessarily loyal to any particular ethnic group or natural heritage. Whereas previous generations learned from the traditions of their fathers and their ideas were filtered through these traditions, the fatherless generation is not so limited when seeking out sources for knowledge and wisdom. Information is accumulated and distributed without reference to any cultural framework, and the absence of influence from the culture of fathers allows the fatherless to be unaccountable to any clear or distinct standards.

The business realm has tapped into the needs of the fatherless generation to develop products that both create a unique identity for the individual, branded with the eponymous "I," "my," and "you," while connecting the individual simultaneously to a global community. The success of these products feeds the duality of the orphan culture. Privacy is a cornerstone of the need for protection, and yet it is balanced against the need for provision, the cornerstone of which is community. Social networking sites such as "MySpace" and "Facebook" are at once private and public. "YouTube" is simultaneously profoundly intimate and totally exhibitionist. Such paradoxes have no rational explanation in the paradigm of the previous generation. Yet, these venues for "sharing" are indispensable to the spread of this generation's culture. The fatherless generation has embraced this model of contradiction, because it makes complete sense within their imperatives of provision and protection.

Lacking stability and predictability in their relationships, the fatherless generation searches for intimacy. As divorce has introduced them to new siblings and stepparents, this generation has had to learn to become a brother or sister to strangers. Family has become an amorphous concept, superficial and highly changeable. These highly variable circumstances have resulted in a deep yearning for a place of belonging and for identity. These experiences have yielded the simultaneous and contradictory desires for privacy and recognition. This generation tends to fear anonymity; so they are inclined to tell the virtual world all of the inane details of their lives, except the details that actually matter, since they also cling fiercely to a desire for privacy. In this vein, celebrities, eager for an expanded fan base, will inform millions about what they had for lunch at their favorite restaurant and tearfully plead to the same audience for the respect of their privacy when going through an agonizing divorce.

The generation's interests in products and services also follow these lines. Electronic games provide them with entertainment at a level of human interaction defined only by their desire and personal boundaries. Ultimate control in the cyber world means that, despite monsters and dangers to their avatar, there is no danger of rejection and abandonment.

MATRIARCHY, A CULTURE OF SURVIVAL

With the absence of fathers, mothers have become the dominant cultural influence upon succeeding generations. Mothers are left to the task of raising children by themselves without much in the way of meaningful help from others. Whereas a father's role is to confirm a child's identity and impart a sense of purpose and destiny, the broken family imparts mainly the culture of survival.

The common reality that faces single mothers is a lack of resources. Throughout the world, families headed by women are preoccupied with the daily struggle for provision and protection. This reality further reinforces the orphan mentality, which substitutes a destiny dominated by the imperatives of provision and protection.

The foundation of our relationship to God the Father, and the foundation of our destiny as children of God, is the relationship of fathers and sons. Therefore, a matriarchal society is an unacceptable alternative to the pandemic of fatherlessness.

THE IMPACT ON GLOBAL SOCIETY

The pervasive influence of the fatherless generation upon global culture is measurable in the way it has begun to reshape the major systems of society throughout the world. It is on track to become the dominant influence shaping the future of these systems. Although it is still in its infancy, its influence is nevertheless unmistakable in global arenas such as commerce, politics, and religion.

COMMERCE

The generation of the fatherless is at the center of commercial innovation and is the driving force of consumerism. In past decades of fast-rising consumerism, the fatherless generation was abandoned by busy parents and assuaged with the most popular forms of electronic entertainment. Single mothers were overwhelmed with the demands on their time and could do little more than meet the basic needs of their children. The "latchkey kid" became a subset of this generation. One consequence of this was that this generation became personally familiar with technology. First, it was a means of entertaining themselves; then it became a way to surpass their parents' acquisition of material wealth.

Electronics and technology became part of their identity. The latest advancements in entertainment and computer technology have produced billion-dollar industries, supported almost entirely by the demand of the fatherless generation. Not only did this generation spawn the advancement of this technology, their familiarity with the workings of the computer and its potential for profit had much to do with the development of online commerce.

With the rapid expansion of commerce related to the Internet, the fatherless generation has become one of the most financially successful demographics in the world. Before the advent of the requisite technology, it was hard to imagine such a large number of young people being so financially powerful. They succeeded in bypassing the apprenticeship system, which was the traditional pathway to wealth and position in previous generations. Neither did they have to wait for the deaths of their parents to inherit large amounts of money with which to build their own fortunes.

They used the monetary freedom to create new areas of business that are compatible with their culture—primarily in the business of information. The Internet itself, together with its related infrastructure, represents a vast distribution network for the flow of information. Fortunes continue to be made through further development and refinement of the Internet.

With the spoils of their enterprises, but without the benefit of a connection to fathers, the newly wealthy fatherless do not have long-term strategies in mind. One of the results of this development is that older generations continue to invest in the industries they understand and helped develop, whereas the newly wealthy generation has succeeded in creating a separate and distinct economy. Although this division is in the early stages, its continuing development will have far-reaching consequences that will manifest in growing unemployment and in economic polarization.

ENVIRONMENTAL POLICY

The closest thing to a common spiritual belief among the fatherless generation is the conviction that the environment needs to be protected. Environmentalism appeals to this generation, because of their need for security in their provision. This generation views the planet as the source of all provision, since there is no defined concept of an inheritance from a previous generation. Generally, they consider the environmental policy of the previous generation as rapacious and have characterized these environmentally harmful policies as the result of being motivated by the desire for financial gain. They see the previous generation's desire for profitability as having stripped future generations of an inheritance of the planet's resources.

In opposition to the environmental policies of the past, the fatherless generation tends to be motivated by more utilitarian gains. In the extreme, this generation will place the welfare of mother nature above that of an individual or group, in furtherance of "the greater good." To this generation, one of the most appealing aspects of the effort to protect the environment is that it affords them the feeling of passing on an inheritance to future generations that is compatible with their motivation for self-preservation, but requires only a vicarious commitment to future generations.

Having maligned the previous generation's environmental policy as contrary to these goals, this type of environmental policymaking tends to lack the consideration of traditional forms of energy supply and production. It is a common approach to analysis in this generation: once the group agrees that the perceived ill was the product of the previous generation's conduct, it typically feels no obligation to justify its proposed alternatives. It is then free to propose any solution, viewing criticism as the predictable reaction of the existing, and failed, authority structure. By discrediting the present generation, it assumes a near-total freedom to propose alternatives with impunity. The result is a policy driven by such operative terms as "renewable," "sustainable," "environmentally friendly," and the like, and solutions to the problems of man's misuse and abuse of the environment that may disregard related costs or the effectiveness of the proposed solutions.

THE CHURCH

The widest chasms between the generation of the fatherless and previous generations exist in their views of religion. Institutional religion is based on tradition and practices that have been elevated to the status of sacred writ, simply because they are customary ways in which Scripture has been interpreted. However, the fatherless generation is unbound from the traditions of their fathers and views these traditions with suspicion.

The younger generation does not have the same need to attend a religious service. The fatherless generation has previously unfathomable access to information via the World Wide Web. Unlike previous generations, the fatherless generation does not go to church to obtain its information on religious subjects, and the view of the local pastor is not necessarily the view of the congregation as a whole. Religious practices have maintained some appeal by the continuing agreement of the majority of the religious community, but the young people who attend religious services do not necessarily hold the same views on religious subjects as the preacher or the older church constituency. The conduct of the younger generation on key issues, such as co-habitation, the use of drugs and alcohol, and general social norms shows an astonishingly wide gulf between the two generations within the same church denominations.

Some churches have adapted by effectively creating two congregations: one for the older generation and one for the younger generation. Nearly everything about these two expressions is radically different. This divided house acknowledges the rift between the generations and yet further separates them.

AN AD HOC SPIRITUALITY

To avoid irrelevance, the churches that have large numbers of attendance have messages that are custom tailored to placate the fatherless culture. These messages are a blend of self-help psychology and motivational speeches, designed to impart information on achieving financial success and maintaining healthy lifestyles. They are market-sensitive messages designed around consumer preferences and have no actual spiritual relevance. However, they seem the perfect blend for the fatherless generation who are inclined to look to church for information on lifestyle issues.

Although on the surface it appears that this generation is driven by consumerism, it is true, nevertheless, that it has a deep longing for spiritual truth. It has searched for religious truth and has great stores of information on religious matters. Yet, it lacks the clarity of the truth. Absent guidance and instruction, members of this generation are likely to seek only for specific needs, but do not understand the overarching principles that form the framework for understanding the specific issues.

They have generally abandoned traditional Christianity, having associated it with hurtful experiences from their childhood, since many of this generation have come from broken families who were members of religious denominations. They have seen the failure of the practice of religion to influence the conduct of their parents in areas of familial stability and the frequency of divorce among religious and nonreligious people alike.

My Father! My Father!

CHAPTER 3

A New Ethical and Moral Basis

Continuing the discussion of the effects of the fatherless culture, it is important to note that the fatherless generation operates from a unique moral perspective. The moral and spiritual convictions of this generation are not generally influenced by any prevailing Christian worldview. Instead, they tend to arise from highly personal convictions that come from within the spheres of their own experiences. Their standards and the choices they reflect are commonly in opposition to the standards of the older generation.

Some of the common points of disagreement between the generations include their views on abortion and premarital sex. Whereas the older generation may consider abortion a hideous sin, the younger generation tends to regard it as purely a matter of personal choice. And, whereas the older generation would have been scandalized by allegations of premarital sex, the younger generation is likely to have had multiple sexual partners prior to marriage.

The fundamental change between the views of the generations is a change from societal standards related to an overall worldview, to a highly individualized standard. This new standard applies beyond the religious context to virtually every form of interaction. One example of this clash between cultures occurred recently in relation to the music industry. The Napster case raised the question of whether personal moral convictions should overrule an existing social standard. Specifically, the question was whether the existing social standard of paying for music should give way to the next generation's view that music should be free.

Through the eyes of the younger generation, free music downloads were an entitlement. Those engaging in "music sharing" argued that, from the time they were children, marketers have enticed them to buy products by giving them free gifts. They cited examples of the collaboration between movie studios, soft drink companies, and hamburger chains and the campaigns designed to both bring children into the movie theaters and to sell products, all as part of a single, overall marketing strategy. The generation argued that companies had traditionally given them trinkets to induce them to purchase their products. In exchange, they bought an array of related merchandise.

Since this was the culture in which they grew up, they expected music artists and the record companies to provide them with the music for free, while they anticipated paying for tickets to live concerts, where they would also be enticed to buy all types of related merchandise. They cited the fact that many famous artists also created clothing lines and accessories designed to benefit from the public appeal of the artists.

The older generation, on the other hand, argued that the artists were entitled to profit from the sale of the songs themselves and that the taking without payment was a crime. Although the case itself was resolved in favor of maintaining the traditional view, its impact brought to light the thinking of an entire generation. Moreover, this clash had the effect of fundamentally changing the music industry. Now, for a nominal fee, consumers may elect to purchase only the song they choose and many popular artists distribute their music free over the Internet while making considerable revenues from ticket sales to live concerts and having become recognized brands for a wide range of consumer products.

FATHERLESSNESS IN THE BLACK CHURCH

The fatherless culture's impact on churches in the United States has been different in large predominantly Black or predominantly White churches, having followed the needs of the fatherless culture unique to each of these communities. The message in the larger Black churches has evolved from the days of the civil rights movement to the present. During the civil rights movement, the Black church played a key role in transitioning Black society from virtual exclusion to a greater inclusion within the nation. Black leaders from the older generation were both religious and political leaders who attempted to play a fatherly role from within the church.

The institutional Black church accepted these leaders as both religious and political, conferring an extraordinary status to them within the Black community. The term "reverend" was applied as readily to a preacher as to a politician. The principle job of the preacher-politician was to negotiate with the central government on behalf of the Black community over a wide range of social issues and empowerment initiatives. This model changed as Black society itself made the long journey from mere survival to the presidency of the United States of America.

Along the way, Black society has undergone profound and irreversible changes. The society has remained fatherless, even in its evolution. The roles of preachers and politicians have been largely separated as a result of the overall change in Black society. The preacher is no longer required to be a politician, and the culture of the orphan has changed the message of the preacher from an emphasis on political enfranchisement to financial empowerment, with the Black church as the purveyor of the message. On Sunday mornings in large Black churches, the message from the pulpit is as much about financial prosperity as it is about faith. The teachings of Jesus are typically reduced to statements that can be used to motivate the audience toward financial gain.

However, beyond the desire for financial empowerment, there is a yearning for a connection to eternal truths emerging within Black society. A solid middle class has arisen, and it is leading the way toward a serious inquiry into spiritual truth and practices. Many voices are now asking questions of profound spiritual depth for which there are no obvious answers. This search will continue beyond the boundaries of Black society itself. As the changes continue, the younger generation of Black people will continue to defy the standards by which their forebears lived.

Older generations of Black people felt limited by issues of race, education, and finances. Younger Black people are throwing off those limitations and seeking answers beyond them. This act yields tremendous potential for change, not just in the Black church, but also in Black society as a whole.

FATHERLESSNESS IN WHITE MEGACHURCHES

In contrast to Black society, which is a fatherless culture because the majority of children are born to single parents, children in White society become orphans primarily as a result of divorce. Although the need for financial empowerment is great among White orphans, the need is greater yet in Black society, and White orphans tend to have greater success in overcoming the obstacles to financial prosperity than orphans who are Black. However, because of the abandonment and neglect that White orphans experience through the breakup of their families, their social training is often deficient. A variety of solutions have proliferated to try and remedy this deficiency.

Many White evangelical or charismatic Christians go to church on Sundays to be instructed in good manners and social graces. Television programs and social network sites offer advice on everything from dating and cooking to child rearing. One of the sources that provides this form of remedial information is the White megachurch. Unlike the Black church, which concentrates its messages on financial empowerment, the White counterpart offers information on a wider range of subjects.

The Sunday morning experience is an attempt to compensate for the loss of fathers, resulting in the loss of culture. Churches, therefore, provide opportunities for social, financial, and political networking. The problem, however, is that it is a gathering of orphans who are then being instructed by orphans. Although this exchange lacks the objectivity that might otherwise make it useful, it feels useful by the mere fact that the information appeals to the imperatives of provision and protection, in the form that is important to the congregation.

THE FATHERLESS AS RELIGIOUS POSTMODERNISTS

Another permutation of the fatherless culture that has arisen within a religious context is the religious postmodernists, who have their own distinct point of view. They have largely rejected the emphases on financial empowerment and social manners as part of their overall rejection of the church system. Their beliefs are formulated in the more general view of the failure of the systems of modern society that is held by postmodernists. Like their secular postmodern cousins, they reject the validity of all things labeled as modernist and have an abiding faith in the "emerging church."

By pointing to the obvious failures of church movements in general, religious postmodernists take to themselves the right to decide the form of all things religious, including the redefinition of God. They have managed to fashion a god to their own liking. The resulting god has none of the characteristics of the fathers they despise and exhibits the behaviors that are socially acceptable and nonthreatening. Such a god never disciplines, nor requires accountability. That god believes in the inherent goodness of man and always interprets man's behavior through the lenses of altruism.

Through this lens, the person who has rejected all the evils of modernism, such as racism, economic colonialism, and exploitation of nature and is laboring to create a society based on fair trade, green technology, and a zero carbon footprint is one who possesses all the qualities of an evolved human. The religious postmodernist is a person who has no need to be accountable. Whatever that person does is motivated by the highest of human ideals and will create a world the way God intended it in the beginning.

An essential characteristic of religious postmodernists as a group is that they have replaced the image of a father with that of the group. The group is characterized by the lack of confrontation and the constant search for consensus. They may accept a father figure as a "mentor." However, the mentor's input is limited to suggestions, which they are free to accept or reject at will. The mentor is always on trial, and his actions are scrutinized and compared to the fathers who failed that generation.

The scope of the religious postmodernists' influence upon the church culture of their generation will emerge with greater clarity over time.

A Unified Global Culture has Arisen

Although the culture of the fatherless has permeated human society, it has largely gone unnoticed. It is forming itself into a new global order whose effects are everywhere. Yet the underlying cause has remained unnoticed and unidentified. This generation typically derives its information from global sources and understands how the greater systems upon which human life depends are becoming integrated seamlessly into a common global order. They view national concerns according to how they affect this global order, and their loyalties are shifting from national preoccupations to a global outlook.

Correspondingly, a global culture is forming. It is presently linked to the creation, storage, and distribution of information. Access to the Internet has permitted this generation to peer into some of the deepest secrets of the world's political and financial empires. Because this generation of fatherless people has transferred their sense of responsibility to a global community, they do not tend to observe restraint in distributing the information they gather to a worldwide audience.

As mentioned previously, the orphan culture of this generation is driven by the twin imperatives of the search for provision and protection. The orphan relies upon no one but himself, and believes that his future is of his own making. He has received no inheritance of value from previous generations and does not feel any measure of obligation to endow future generations. In his self-reliance, the orphan never fully trusts any other person, and is committed to his own well-being as his first priority. He is governed by the fear of not having enough to provide for all his needs and of never being good enough to meet the expectations of others. An orphan is, therefore, always insecure about the motives of others. His destiny is defined by his skills, and he does not view his life's purpose as part of an unfolding reality. His destiny can only be calculated to augment his ability to supply what he needs, and his success is measured in terms of his accomplishments.

The orphan has no sense of a divine calling defining his destiny. Whenever he thinks of his relationship to God, he automatically defaults to a standard of performance. He wants to know what price he must pay to obtain the favor of God, and even when he embraces a theology of grace, he still functions out of a mentality of works. His religious faith seems to have almost no impact upon these fundamental tenants of his culture. He lives between the natural world and the spiritual world and manages to maintain his mental health by keeping these two worlds completely separate.

The rise of this culture, its pervasiveness, and its seeming inexorable momentum raises many questions regarding man, his existence, and his destiny: From where did the culture of the orphan originate, and how has it come to be so completely pervasive? Has humankind always been like this? Is this culture the inevitable result of man having evolved out of primordial substances to become the dominant fearsome predator?

Perhaps more pressing are the questions of a better way: Is there a way to a nobler existence? If so, was there ever an alternative vision that defined man's existence and purpose? And, can he find his way home—perhaps even to his Father's house?

My Father! My Father!

CHAPTER 4

The Spirit of the Orphan

...but from the beginning it was not so.[9]

The fall of man has been far more precipitous than religious traditions have taught. When God created man, His original intent was to create a son, whose purpose in creation was to represent God, his Father. The fall both separated the son from the father and changed the culture of man from that of a son to that of an orphan. This resulted in the introduction of the fatherless culture, a distinct and unique culture to the earth, and frustrated God's original purpose for creating man.

The fatherless culture is more than the impetus for the commission of sinful acts. It is an altered state of thinking and acting based upon a fundamental change in the way man perceives reality.

As told in Scripture, this culture has existed and has grown to its present expression from the beginning of human history. This was not the nature of the relationship between God and man that God originally intended; as Jesus once remarked, "from the beginning it was not so."[10]

ADAM WAS THE SON OF GOD

This truth has been unequivocally stated in Scripture: God decided to make Adam in His own image and likeness;[11] and, therefore, Adam was created as "the son of God."[12] However, most religious traditions choose to see man as a creation that God made for the purpose of worshiping Him. They present man as this lowly creature who, in an unimaginable act of collusion with Satan, became an unconscionable ingrate. As punishment, the Creator banished him from paradise and condemned him to death and hell until the time God would choose to save him. In these traditions, man is thereafter required to do things to please God, or else suffer the consequence of an eternal hell. This story contains some elements that are true, but is far from the truth of man's relationship to God.

A far greater purpose for the creation of man is revealed in the preparations God made for the advent of man into creation. God designed a world that would renew itself for a very long time, indicating that His purposes for the creation of man were meant to unfold over many millennia and would include a vast number of human beings. God established an entire economy to provide for His sons. He created "seed-bearing plants and trees on the land that bear fruit with seed in it, according to their various kinds."[13] He created "living creatures according to their kinds: livestock, creatures that move along the ground, and wild animals, each according to its kind."[14] Then, after He created man, He declared that these things were intended for man's provision:

> *I give you every seed-bearing plant on the face of the whole earth and every tree that has fruit with seed in it. They will be yours for food. And to all the beasts of the earth and all the birds of the air and all the creatures that move on the ground—everything that has the breath of life in it—I give every green plant for food.*[15]

God created a son in God's own image and in His own likeness. The purpose for the creation of man is contained in this fact.

MAN IS SPIRIT

On the sixth day of creation, after God had created everything necessary to sustain human life, He created man. God first declared His intent to make man in His own image, in His own likeness.[16] Then, He executed that intention exactly: "So God created man in his own image, in the image of God he created him; male and female he created them."[17] God fashioned the form of man out of clay, from the dust of the ground, and He inserted into this form a spirit, which came out of the very person of God. Thus, God made man's true nature that of spirit and a son of God.

God is the Father of our spirits. "[W]e have all had human fathers who disciplined us and we respected them for it. How much more should we submit to the Father of our spirits and live!"[18] Man is the only creation that may claim to be the son of God. Sonship is in regard to man's spirit, not his body.[19] Our physical body is not the part of our being that is like God, as a son is like his father. God created the form that the man's spirit would occupy out of the most common elements found on the earth. The body, fashioned from the dust of the ground, was meant to die,[20] to be discarded and raised as a spiritual body.[21] Moreover, God does not discriminate in the sonship of humans based on their physical attributes. We are all sons without regard for race, bloodline, or gender.[22]

When God imparted His Spirit into man out of His own person, He created a being that was compatible with the nature of God.[23] The intent of God was to make a son who would be in kind and nature like God. God designed him so that God could communicate with him and direct him, and he would respond because he was, by nature, like God. God then placed this spiritual being into the previously formed creation.

As a spiritual entity, Adam was an alien to the earth. The origin of his spirit is from the very person of God, making man unique among all created beings. Humans are an entirely different species from either those that exist in the heavens, such as angels and

35

demons, or the animals that occupy the physical realm. God has never included any other creature in the designation "sons of God."[24]

One of the consequences of the fall was man's loss of ability to hear God. It was always the intention of God to fellowship with His son, Spirit to spirit. "The Spirit himself testifies with our spirit that we are God's children."[25] For God to communicate with man, the human spirit must be compatible with the Spirit of God. Otherwise, God could only communicate with man through symbols, types, shadows, and copies.

After the fall, man's own perception of good and evil replaced God's impartation—which man received during his daily visit with God. Man's spirit became insensitive to the voice of God, and he was no longer informed through his interactions with God. Although God would continue to speak to humankind, man's new culture of heeding his own wisdom had taken root. From that time on, man's own voice would constantly compete with the voice of God.

Being the son of God, man was designed to function in tandem with God. He was to be the agent through whom God would put on display His own nature. But, the introduction of a radically distinct culture of independence in the fall would continue to oppose the culture of man as a son.

SONS ARE RULERS

"When God created man, he made him in the likeness of God. He created them male and female and blessed them. And when they were created, he called them 'man.'"[26] "Adam" is the proper name God gave to his first son, but "adam" also means "man," in the general sense.[27] It is appropriate, therefore, to refer to the general condition of mankind in terms that apply to "Adam," and references herein to the rule of man or the fall of man apply to Adam and Eve, because Adam and Eve were both the sons of God.

God put man in creation to manage an order that God had established in the earth prior to making man. The order of living things was this:

Then God said, "Let the land produce vegetation: seed-bearing plants and trees on the land that bear fruit with seed in it, according to their various kinds." And it was so. …And God said, "Let the water teem with living creatures, and let birds fly above the earth across the expanse of the sky." …God blessed them and said, "Be fruitful and increase in number and fill the water in the seas, and let the birds increase on the earth." …And God said, "Let the land produce living creatures according to their kinds: livestock, creatures that move along the ground, and wild animals, each according to its kind." And it was so.[28]

God made man and declared, "let them rule over the fish of the sea and the birds of the air, over the livestock, over all the earth, and over all the creatures that move along the ground."[29] Even the lights in the expanse of the sky were part of this order. God created them to not only separate day and night, but also serve as signs to designate the changing seasons, as well as days and years.[30] God intended them not only to show the cycles of changing years and epochs, but also to signal the introduction of heavenly mandates into time.[31] Before Adam sinned, he was living out the destiny to rule over the earth as the son of God.[32]

In committing rule to Adam, God intended to place a son in creation that, in his rule, would be as a surrogate of his Father. When God created the earth, He extended his own rule over this new realm. He, therefore, owed a duty to either rule it himself or to do so through a surrogate.

All forms of rule express the nature and the imperatives of the sovereign. Accordingly, exact representation is an essential element of the rule of an agent of the sovereign. Since rule on the earth would, of necessity, display the nature of God, it was essential that God's representative on the earth be one who understood the nature of God. Man's rule in the earth, therefore, had to be the exact manner in which God himself would rule. Otherwise, the form of rule of the earth would not represent the rule of God.

Only a creature specifically made for this purpose could fulfill this role, and only a son of God could represent the rule of God accurately. Inasmuch as the son himself is a "[partaker] of the divine nature" of his father,[33] a son would know and understand the nature of the Father.

Only a son could impart the underlying culture of the father's rule to the domain over which the son has been established to rule. As sovereign over the earth, Adam was tasked with establishing a form of order that was a mirror image of the existing order of heaven itself. He was required to translate the order of God as it existed in heaven into the earth. Both the form of his rule and the spirit of his rule were to be representations of the existing heavenly order.

By contrast, the delegated rule of a servant would be distinctly different from the rule of a son. The son knows the intent of his father's heart and is the heir of all that the father possesses. A servant, on the other hand, can only execute what he has been told. The servant has no capacity to represent God, because he is not a "partaker" of the same nature of the Father, in the way of a son. The servant is obligated to view everything from a servant's viewpoint and not from the point of view of an heir. The heir seeks the advancement of his father's interests, because they are the same as his own. A servant is preoccupied with fulfilling his duty. The heir owns the whole house, whereas the servant performs the duties associated with his station within the house.

Likewise, angels are ministering servants who serve the interests of God and the sons of God. Whereas, sons are capable of portraying the nature and character of their father; a son is a personal representation of his father. Therefore, God did not commit the rule of the earth to angels, because although angels are great in power, they are nevertheless servants.[34]

God's Sovereign Nature

All forms of government are rooted in some concept of sovereignty. Historic forms of sovereignty are mainly monarchical

38

and over time have ruled nations through dynasties. In modern times, however, sovereignty, being described as the source of the authority to govern, has been reassigned as arising from the people or from the state. Regardless of the form that sovereignty takes, the administration associated with the execution of the sovereign's power is inevitably through delegates. The associated bureaucracies are required to translate the culture of the sovereign into practical administration and are, therefore, the face that the sovereign presents to the governed.

For example, in the case where the people are the sovereign, a common complaint is that the agents of the administration do not reflect properly the ideals of the people, which is often the source of the people's discontent. The search is always for representatives of the government who accurately portray the collective culture of the people as sovereign. In comparison, the state as sovereign has routinely produced an administration characterized by contempt for individual freedoms and aspirations. Maintaining the power of the monolithic state has been characteristic of the nature of these administrations. In every case, the sovereign is best served by an administration in which the culture of the sovereign is most accurately portrayed.

The same is true of the delegated rule of a monarch. When a ruler sends his son to a new domain, he does so to bring the culture of the house into that place. The son is a viceroy of his father, the king.

Historically, the arrival of a viceroy signaled the serious intent of a conquering king to "civilize" new territories and peoples by imposing the king's laws, institutions, practices, and customs upon the conquered people. The term "civilization" is often used to describe the process of imposing a standard of civil order upon an existing culture. As an example, when a more powerful nation subdues a less powerful nation, it is the habit of the powerful to impose its laws, institutions, and customs upon the conquered people. The intent is to create uniformity throughout the empire. The weaker nation is "civilized" to the standards of the more powerful nation. The result is that the conquered nation experiences a change in its institutions and practices. The old order is swept away, and the new order is implemented.

When the viceroy was a son of the ruling king, there could be no mistake regarding the intention of the king to bring those territories under the rule of the throne and to infuse the culture of the conquered people with the culture of their new king. Inasmuch as the king sent his son, it was to be clearly understood that it was the undisguised intent of the monarch to give his highest priority to imposing the way of life already established in his kingdom upon his new citizens.

Being raised by his father, the son was fully aware of the culture of his father and of the kingdom. It would be inconceivable that the son would deviate substantially from the norms of the court of his father. The son was, after all, actually ruling for himself, because eventually he would be king. By accurately representing his father's government, the son might insure the continuity of the kingdom itself. Great noble families often ruled kingdoms for centuries in this way. Monarchical rule is, by nature, trans-generational.

By contrast, a servant or slave has neither the culture of the father, to rule as the father would rule, nor the inclination to act for the benefit of future generations of rulers. Nobility is distinguished by the sense of continuity through multiple generations. The conservation of power over multiple generations produces a distinctly different culture of rule than what may be accomplished in a single lifetime or for the benefit of an individual.

God's Representative Is His Son

Adam was sent in the place of God the Father, a viceroy of the Kingdom of Heaven. The apostle Paul wrote, "For this reason I kneel before the Father, *from whom his whole family in heaven and on earth derives its name.*"[35] When a father sends a son into a new territory, the family extends itself through the son into that domain. When God put His Son into the earth, the Kingdom of Heaven existed in both heaven and earth. Although the headquarters remained in heaven, the rule of the Kingdom was now on earth in the same fashion in which it was in heaven. Although the domain of heaven and earth are markedly different, the character of rule is the same, since all forms of rule reflect the character of the sovereign.

As the delegated ruler in the earth, Adam's mandate was to represent his Father. By making his delegate a son, in the image and likeness of his God, God ensured there was no impediment to Adam's ability to accurately represent the nature of his Father.

Exact representation of another requires sameness of being, and accurate positioning with respect to the one who is being represented. Adam was, in nature, a "partaker of the divine nature," since his being was issued out of the person of God. The term "son" is the appropriate designation, since Adam was a spirit whose origin was out of the person of God. Although God implanted His spirit into a "house of mortal clay,"[36] man's essential nature remained a spirit. God designed man with this sameness of spirit with the intention of assigning him the role of exactly representing God in the earth.

When God placed Adam into the earth, He was accurately positioning Adam as the head of the government of the Kingdom of Heaven in the domain of earth. The attack upon Adam by Satan was targeted to disrupt the accuracy of his positioning. Adam's commission to rule the earth and to "subdue it" was a grant of authority from God[37]—it cannot function independently of God's influence, since Adam was the viceroy to rule in God's stead. Satan could not affect the reality of Adam's sonship, since that was settled by God's decision both to create Adam as His son and to regard him as His son. Adam, however, was vulnerable in the matter of the choices that informed the character of his rule. He could rule as a son, controlled by the nature of his Father resident within him, or he could elect to discard that restraint and rule independently, as he saw fit. When Adam chose the latter, his rule devolved into his personal pursuit for provision and protection.

In the rule of Adam, the earth was meant to see an exact display of the nature of God himself. Adam's rule would portray the order and the character of God. The result would be that the same order of relationships that exists in heaven would be on display on the earth through God's son, Adam. Under the rule of the son, all who lived on the earth would experience the goodness of God. This is seen in Jesus' declaration of the purpose for which He had been given to the earth. "[Y]our kingdom come, your will be done on earth as it is in heaven."[38] When God made Adam, God intended that the Kingdom would exist on the earth as it did in heaven, the will of God would be done on the earth as it was in heaven, and all of the benefits associated with the rule of God would come upon the earth through Adam.

The announcement of the birth of Jesus was the declaration of God's intent to restore the government of heaven to the earth in the form of His Kingdom and to invite humans to seek the good order and peace of His rule over their lives.[39] God was resuming the pursuit of His original plan, which He first revealed through Adam. Isaiah prophesied the coming of Jesus and the restoration of the government of the Kingdom of Heaven when he wrote, "For to us a child is born, to us a son is given, and the government will be on his shoulders."[40]

THE SAME ORDER IN EARTH AND HEAVEN

God created the earth to house physical allegories of heaven's transcendent qualities. "For since the creation of the world God's invisible qualities—his eternal power and divine nature—have been clearly seen, being understood from what has been made, so that people are without excuse."[41] God often chooses to explain great truths of heaven through references to the plant and animal kingdom. So, a son looks like his father, and plants and animals reproduce according to their own kind. These physical representations act as veiled types and shadows that reflect the actual order of heaven.

Human relationships, however, are the most consistently utilized format through which God explains Himself. God created Adam as His son and is, therefore, in the role of Father. Adam was given spirit out of the being of God, and the place of a son is created. Son, therefore, is the appropriate designation for that which issues out of another. Adam is then put into a deep sleep and God takes a part of his body and forms another body out of it. God formed Eve out of Adam; and when God presented her to him, Adam declared that she is "bone of my bones and flesh of my flesh; she shall be called 'woman,' for she was taken out of man."[42] Eve also was given a spirit from God, as is the case with all humanity. Since Adam, humans have had this dual identity, since their bodies are the products of the seed of their fathers, incubated in their mother's wombs. However, all human spirits are original gifts from God;[43] all humans are born of flesh and may be born again of spirit.[44] Likewise, the relationship between a husband and wife is part of God's divine order and explains certain heavenly truths.

Paul taught that God designed this type and shadow to explain the mystery of Christ and the Church.[45] By making the woman's body out of the man, God created a physical representation of how God Himself created man, by giving him an endowment of spirit out of God's own person. Eve was, therefore, the first son of Adam, since God chose to fashion her body out of Adam's flesh and bone. God deliberately made woman this way as the foundation of the essential character of heavenly government.

Not only did God make the physical creation to be an allegory of the order of heaven, but He arranged His government as a form of rule designed for representation, namely, the one who had authority is required to train, instruct, and model for the one who is under authority the proper order of rule. In due course, the one under authority becomes mature and can replicate the same order of rule in which he had been trained within the spheres of his authority. In this model, the father would have trained the son to exactly represent the father. The influence of the father would be pervasive, yet he would not immediately control all the spheres and domains over which his sons would rule. The father's contribution would be the creation of a culture and the sons would have executive decision making over their spheres of authority.

As a woman, Eve was both the son of God and the son of Adam. Eve's administration was meant to display in part the authority God gave to Adam. With respect to Adam, Eve was flesh of his flesh and bone of his bone and was designed to function with him. Yet, she was assigned a function that was distinct from anything he could possibly do himself. Although he contained the seed from which all the nations would come, without Eve the earth would remain unpopulated. Her role as his son included her unique position as his wife. These twin roles were not incompatible inasmuch as the role of son refers to the capacity of representation, while the role of wife defines the form of that representation.

Without Eve's administration, Adam's authority would remain with him alone. By creating Eve out of Adam, God made it possible for them to have the closest relationship possible between two human beings. This was meant to portray the type of relationship possible between God and man on the basis of one Spirit to another spirit. For "he that is joined unto the Lord is one spirit,"[46] and "[t]he Spirit himself testifies with our spirit that we are God's children."[47] By making her distinct from Adam, however, God endowed Eve with the capacity to uniquely represent Adam.

Although Adam and Eve were separate creatures with individual identities, they were designed by God to function interdependently and without competition. There was, therefore, no need for equality, since equality and fairness are the ways in which righteousness is described in an environment of competition. However, within the functional context of interdependency, the uniqueness of each person may be fully celebrated. There would be no place for jealousy, envy, and strife, since the ones under authority are indispensable to the display of the culture of those in authority and the true character and intent of those in authority are given the widest possible expression through the administrations of those by whom they are represented.

The effect of Adam's separation from his Father, however, became immediately apparent. All of his relationships were affected by the fall, and the seeds of discord within his relationships flowered fully over the course of human civilization. He rejected the unique relationship with his wife, her sonship, and immediately began to view her as wholly other than himself. Adam changed his perspective from describing Eve as "flesh of my flesh," to "[t]he woman you put here with me," blaming God and Eve for his sin.[48] Having lost his own sonship, Adam stripped Eve of hers in relationship to himself, thus introducing competition and thereby elevating the value of individualism over corpus.

The environment of comparison and competition that Adam's rejection of Eve engendered would have devastating consequences. By the second generation of man, the spirit of genocide was introduced when Cain killed his brother Abel in jealousy.

Adam remained in creation for nearly one thousand years, during which time, the order of human society fully evolved under his rule. Although he sinned and his rule increasingly deviated from his original mandate, God never revoked the authority He gave Adam over creation. Adam was the original father who had talked with God, and he established the fundamental outlines that formed the context of his rule together with the accompanying order of its government.

The form of Adam's government was rooted in the centrality of the role of the father, and the representation of the father's culture through sons. During Adam's lifetime, this form would take on the complexity of family, household, clan, tribe, and nation, as the descendants of a father multiplied in the earth. This form of rule was the optimum form for the maintaining of good order and peace over multiple generations. All of human society was initially based upon this form of order, until the means of traveling widely allowed migration and the intermixing of nations to form alternative social orders.

My Father! My Father!

CHAPTER 5

The Knowledge of Good and Evil

But you must not eat from the tree of the knowledge of good and evil, for when you eat of it you will surely die.[49]

God's nature is to love. Love cannot remain as an unexpressed emotion. If the nature of one is to love, then the mere existence of that nature compels the one possessing it to put it on display. Because God is love, it was always inevitable that He would eventually express His love; and because His love is perfect, His expression of it would also define the nature of love perfectly. That expression would, therefore, involve a creation designed to give expression to the nature of God Himself:

> *...Everyone who loves has been born of God and knows God. Whoever does not love does not know God, because God is love. This is how God showed his love among us: He sent his one and only Son into the world that we might live through him. This is love: not that we loved God, but that [H]e loved us and sent his Son as an atoning sacrifice for our sins. Dear friends, since God so loved us, we also ought to love one another. No one has ever seen God; but if we love one another, God lives in us and his love is made complete in us.*[50]

The facets of the love of God come together and are seen through the Son. All who individually represent different aspects of the love of God as parts of the body of the Son are destined to be presented together as one corporate entity—the Body of Christ.

Satan's Argument

When God announced His choice for His heirs, Satan formed a rebellion against the choice. The act of rebelling called into question God's righteousness, implying that He made an erroneous choice when He chose man as His heir. The argument is simple: if the creature is unworthy, then God's choice of him is erroneous and the argument of Satan that the angels and Satan were unfairly passed over would be tantamount to God having made a mistake. If God were to have made a mistake, then all claims to His flawless wisdom and perfection would be spurious. Even if God did not recant His choice of man and choose angels instead, if His choice were proven to be mistaken, then Satan's effort to unseat Him would have a chance of succeeding. God could have responded by annihilating Satan and his angels, but doing so would have left unanswered the question of the righteousness of God's choice. He, therefore, created the earth and man in order to resolve this question.

Satan came into the Garden of Eden, motivated by this prior history, with the intent of engaging the conflict on the earth. Angels enjoy significant advantages over man when they come into the domain of man. They have prior knowledge derived from their previous places in heaven together with the advantage of being spirit beings in a natural world. Therefore, God has limited the manner in which Satan and his angels could engage man.

The earth was created to host the existence of man, whom God called His son. This is "the beginning" referred to in Genesis 1:1, "In the beginning God created the heavens and the earth." Since God alone is the Beginning and the End,[51] everything else that exists God created.[52] The angels and all other creations in heaven preexisted man and this physical creation.

As mentioned previously, God never referred to an angel as a son and created angels in anticipation of their service to the sons.[53] The creation of the angels predated that of man, because God created all angels as servants, first to God and subsequently to man. The order of created things shows God's plan that He intended to put into effect, at the appropriate time, in the sequence of His choosing.

Angels were created into categories of service and are limited in their functioning to their design. As noted earlier, a son, due to his sameness of nature, may represent his father, whereas a servant is designed only to perform a specific task and not for broad and general representation. Some of these categories include warring angels, messenger angels, and angels designed for the holy order of procession when God chooses to reveal Himself to the spirit of man in visions and dreams.[54]

God announced His intention to bring forth a race of beings through which He would put on display the totality of His being according to His eternal plan. It was immediately apparent to the angels—part of the prior creation, of which Satan was the mightiest and most eminent—that this decision would confer the greatest inheritance possible upon a creature. Such a creation would be made a beneficial heir of the nature of God Himself. He would be God's son, created in the image and likeness of God. As the son of God, he would have general authority in heaven and on earth. God's decision to create a race of these creatures was rooted in His nature to love; for God is love.

GOD'S LOVE

God expressed His love by creating man, a being like Him in nature that could choose to inherit the authority of God's Kingdom and extend the rule of heaven to the earth; and by man's rule, God's nature and character, His love, would be fully displayed. Love is inherently vulnerable; it puts one's interest at risk, in the hands of another, while investing faith and hope in the reciprocal affection of the other. The reciprocal nature of love means that love cannot exist if it is not expressed.

The love of God is different from His creative competence or the glory evidenced by the harmonies of divine order. The highest form of God's love is expressed in the desire of the one created to be like God, out of whom he came forth. The term "worship" describes the most complete expression of this desire. Being like God means loving as God loves. It means choosing a path that is part of the full, corporate expression of the love of God to the rest of the world.

Until God created creatures capable of being endowed with His nature, and would reciprocate by embracing the desire to be like Him as their personal choice and would submit their personal desires to the corporate government that would cause them to function in a manner similar to the parts of the human body, the love of God would remain unrevealed. God expressed His love by creating man who, by delegation, could fully express the love of God to all creation.

The full expression of God's love is meant to occur corporately, with each individual being one facet of the larger expression. This corporate expression is built upon the father and son relationship. This relationship is the building block of the family of God, also known as the House of God.

When a house has been built, the creativity that once existed within the designer of the house is outwardly put on display for all to see. The house itself is useful for all that it has been designed to accommodate, and its relevance is determined by its function. The structure's beauty, together with its function, however, confers a measure of honor to its designer that is even greater than may be conferred upon the structure itself. The beauty of the form of the building silently testifies to the creativity and character of the designer.

When man functions as God designed him to function, he confers value to the earth. In that sense he functions as a house. In the beauty of his functioning, however, he testifies to the nature of God, his designer, and the greater glory belongs to God, who made him—"When Christ, who is your life, appears, then you also will appear with him in glory."[55]

"…[J]ust as the builder of a house has greater honor than the house itself. For every house is built by someone, but God is the builder of everything. …And we are his house, if we hold on to our courage and the hope of which we boast."[56] In representing the Father, the son is intimately committed to the Father and derives his identity and his function from the Father. When the son exactly represents the Father, he is doing only what he was designed to do. The beauty of the nature of the Father is displayed through him and he brings glory to the Father in the same way that the house brings glory to the designer. The house is a statement that translates the intangible emotions of the designer into a functional reality.

Man's Choice

However, the essential matter to the conflict between God and Satan is that of man's choice to be like God. In engaging man on this ground, the fallen angels and Satan are unrestrained in the tactics they may employ to separate man from God. All of their efforts are focused upon the ability of man to make choices independently of God.

The seat of man's independence from God is his soul. God endowed man with a spirit so that he might be able to fellowship with God, and God gave him a soul so that he might exercise a meaningful choice to do so—or not.

The soul provided Satan with the richest possibility of engaging man in his effort to prove that the creature was unworthy to be God's son and heir. God had to permit access to the human being through the soul, because the proof that His choice of man as His heir was indeed correct would come when, in spite of the full range of the enemy's attacks against him, he remained faithful and unwavering in his love for and his pursuit of God and would continually present himself as a vessel in whom God can dwell as He wills.

Man's choice, then, establishes the righteousness of God. Thus the Scriptures say, "Be reconciled to God. God made him who had no sin to be sin for us, so that in him we might become the righteousness of God."[57] The war between God and Satan, which began in the heavens, has continued on earth within man's being. The outcome will establish the righteousness of God in His choice, by the undeniable evidence of man choosing to be like his Father in the face of the enemy's most unrelenting pressures. In man's choice, the assertion that God's nature is to love would become a demonstrated reality.

Moreover, by permitting Satan to give full and unrestricted exposure to his nature, evil would be disclosed in all its hideousness. When the process has fully run its course, God can then expunge the taint of sin from the entire creation. With the removal of sin, the authority of death is revoked. Anything that is sinful results in death, whether of human relationships or in practices that defile and corrupt.[58] The rule of sin always leads to death to the thing over which sin presides. But, everything under the rule of love flourishes—even in this present world. When sin is removed and death is destroyed, life in all of its abundance will characterize the rule and reign of God and His sons.[59]

MAN'S NATURE

The human being comprises three parts: the spirit, the soul, and the body.[60] Prior to the fall, man saw everything by the spirit and was in perfect union with God. Man's soul had been in submission to his spirit; his spirit directed his choices.

Satan directed his efforts toward changing the way man saw himself in relationship to God. His efforts were designed to "open the eyes" of the soul.[61] Satan told man that he had secret knowledge of why God restricted man from eating of the tree of the knowledge of good and evil. His assertion was that the fruit of the tree was designed to unlock the hidden knowledge that would permit access into the secrets of God. Satan's effort was to create a means by which man could rule independently of God. Being deceived, man assumed that the creation could exist independent of a divine purpose and would renew itself perpetually. Under the rule of man apart from God, the domain of earth would be severed from the culture of heaven and would exist and be ruled outside the authority of God, subject only to the wisdom of man.

Since the earth was a territory in the domain of the Kingdom of Heaven, God's throne guaranteed its continuity, but if its ruler, mankind, seceded that territory from the rule of heaven, then man's inability to renew the territory would subject it to "the bondage to decay."[62] And the earth would wait in that condition, groaning in anticipation of the sons of God who would liberate it and restore it to the function for which it was designed.[63]

The success of Satan's appeal to Adam's soul would have disastrous consequences for both the man and the earth. Earth would be imprisoned in these consequences until man was redeemed. The consequences themselves would not remain static, but would become progressively more corrupt, ultimately portraying the true nature of evil. However, the redemption of man and the creation would also fully display the love of God. For where sin abounds grace does much more abound.[64]

When the eyes of the soul were opened, man's view of himself and his purpose in creation underwent a complete change. He transitioned from being a son to becoming fatherless; and in that transition, he lost the vision of himself as being spirit, like his Father, and saw himself as flesh.

THEREFORE AN ORPHAN

That transition shifted his perspective from one in which he ruled over creation to merely a survivor. By separating himself from his Father and coming to rely upon himself, he could no longer represent the rule of his Father. All of his assumptions regarding reality, purpose, and destiny changed. He departed from the culture of his Father and began a culture driven by the imperatives of provision and protection.

Immediately after the eyes of his soul were opened, Adam's

actions make clear the transition that occurred. As an orphan, he could no longer rely upon the estate of his Father for support of his rule, because orphans have no fathers. Bereft of the provision and protection of his Father, he immediately set about to supply both needs. He lost the sense of continuity of purpose and began to live for the day. Therefore, he clothed himself and hid from God "among the trees of the garden."[65]

Adam's actions were the result of the new knowledge he had just acquired by eating from the tree of the knowledge of good and evil. The tree was planted in the Garden along with the tree of life, to provide a representation in the earth of the actual choices that already existed, and which man would face. Satan had already chosen independence from God. Man was created with the spirit of God in him so that he would naturally depend upon God for everything that pertained to his existence. As long as man chose to walk in fellowship and communion with God, his supply would be unending and his life would be truly abundant. These two trees— the tree of life and the tree of the knowledge of good and evil— were symbolic of the choices available to man.

The tree of the knowledge of good and evil embodied the alternative to life supported by God. Since God gave "every tree-bearing fruit" to man for food, it is significant that God forbade him the fruit of the tree of the knowledge of good and evil. In contrast, he was free to eat from the fruit of the tree of life, and was only kept from it after he chose to also eat of the tree of the knowledge of good and evil, the fruit of which was the introduction of a new and conflicting basis of life itself.

It was not merely the act of eating the fruit that was sinful. Instead, it was that God established the parameters of choice available to man, symbolized by these trees. The Spirit of God established creation to mirror realities already existing in heaven. These two trees represented the extremes of the patterns of life that the earth was designed to host. They embodied the existing conflict between God and Satan, and were the two extremes of the choice that man's nature would require him to make.

The compendium of knowledge represented by the tree of the knowledge of good and evil was the basis for an alternative reality to man as spirit representing his Father to creation. Instead, the knowledge of the tree offered an order of life in which the creature might live in complete independence from his Creator, like Satan. This independent order obligated the creation to duplicate the functions of God on its own and forge a destiny of his own choosing. This was true of both man and Satan.

The choice of independence would appeal to the soul of man. The knowledge, symbolized by the tree of the knowledge of good and evil, is the result of a process of observation, analysis, comparison, theory, and activity; in a word, reason. Eve observed that the fruit on the tree was "pleasing to the eye,"[66] and she had been told that it was desirable to make her wise. She compared the restraint of God's warning against eating the fruit with the information from Satan to make her choice.

By eating the fruit of the tree, Adam displayed the necessary recklessness that permitted him to throw off the restraint of his Father in order to enter a world in which he was required to supply all of the answers to the question of his being. Upon being presented with a portion of the fruit that his wife had picked, Adam deliberately chose to rebel against the specific instructions of his Father. Then, by reason, the man concluded that his reality was not spirit but flesh; he began to engage that reality by fashioning clothing for his flesh. Whereas, previously, as long as he saw himself as a son to his Father, he accepted the fact that he was a spirit, because his Father was spirit. His flesh was the clothing with which God clothed the spirit, and he was not naked, but was a spirit clothed in flesh.[67] Both Adam and Eve made a conscious and deliberate choice that permanently altered their vision of reality.

Similarly, Adam's perception of God also changed from that of a loving Father to an enemy. It was this change in perception that explains his efforts to evade God by hiding among the trees of the Garden. He would later explain to God that he hid out of the fear that permeated him when he heard the sound of the Lord in the Garden.

When the soul determined man's reality, his rule degenerated to the imperatives of his provision and his protection. At first, after the fall, the only enemy man perceived was God, and provision and protection were rudimentary. He fashioned clothing and he hid. However, within one generation, man would begin to see other men as enemies as well. When he saw man as his enemy, his options for protecting himself would come to include annihilating his enemy. Thus, the fruit of the tree of the knowledge of good and evil would have an ever-expanding field of expression to include war, genocide, and indiscriminant murder. The expression of motivation for provision would expand to include unconscionable and indiscriminant exploitation of the environment and all within it. Only time was required before the full consequences of the decisions of man's soul—to deny the restraints of his Father and to act on his own and for himself—would become evident.

As long as the earth continued to revolve, the gap between the realities as perceived through the spirit and the soul would widen, and the ways of man would depart from the ways of God, until the results of both would be presented in stark contrast at the end of the age.

Along the path of this "long day of dying," God would send the next Adam to restore the vision of the spirit that the first Adam abandoned. An entire race of humans, chosen from all the races that came out of Adam, would reemerge. They would present the alternative that was God's original vision for man, governed by the perspectives of the spirit. This reality would be the fruit of the tree of life, for they would be reconciled to God the Father through Jesus, the Sent One, through whom God would reconcile the world to Himself, "not counting people's sins against them."[68]

CHAPTER 6

A Change from Spirit to Soul

God created man as an expression of Himself that was intended to reside in a venue different from His own. The context for God's decision to make man in His own image and likeness was "so that they may rule over the fish in the sea and the birds in the sky, over the livestock and all the wild animals, and over all the creatures that move along the ground."[69] This is consistent with God's intent to relate to man as a son and His representative, but shows that the sons' representation was to take place on the earth. Therefore, God fashioned the body of man from dust and breathed spirit from His own person into this created form. The result was that man became a "living soul."[70]

The underlying intention of God in putting His son into the earth was to cause Himself to be seen and understood within the natural world. To accomplish this goal, God made a single being composed of three parts: a body, a soul, and a spirit. The body, created of dust, was material and compatible with the physical world. The environment of earth was neither harmful nor detrimental to the human body, but perfectly compatible and supportive to human existence. Indeed, God designed the physical world to be both useful to and harmonious with man's physical form.

The spirit within man, originating out of the person of God as a gift from God Himself, was native to the world of God, that of spirit and of heaven. This aspect of man's being is, therefore, as much at home in the invisible realm of spirits as his body is at home in the natural world.

Within man, the soul bridges the gap between the natural world and that of the spirit. The purpose of the soul is to translate the realm of spirit to the natural. In his exercise of dominion on the earth, man's soul governs the actions of his body. The soul, in turn, is meant to be informed by and obsequious to the spirit of man. Whereas, the spirit of man is the part of man's being that is in close fellowship and communion with God at all times.

Man's soul, then, is meant to interpret and present God's divine nature and eternal purposes to the natural world. The soul itself is a mirror image of man's spirit, meant to function in tandem with the spirit. A similar relationship exists between the Spirit of God and the spirit of man. God imparted His own spirit into the being of man so that the spirit of man could function in perfect harmony with the Spirit of God. The ultimate outworking of this arrangement is that "since the creation of the world God's invisible qualities—[H]is eternal power and divine nature—have been clearly seen, being understood from what has been made."[71] Created in His image and likeness, and designed to present the invisible God to the created world, man is, unquestionably, God's magnum opus—the greatest creation of which God is capable.

The fall destroyed this elegant balance and freed the soul to act independently of the spirit. With this loss of the harmony between soul and spirit, man was unable to enter and remain in God's rest. The saving of one's soul, therefore, is the return of the soul to the rule of the spirit so that man may once again enter God's rest and function in the earth as God originally intended for him. This great task is accomplished progressively over time, being "work[ed] out...with fear and trembling."[72]

SPIRIT, SOUL, AND BODY

The struggle between the two realities centered in soul and spirit has continued from the time of Adam's fall until now. Even

Jesus was not immune to this struggle. As the hour of His death approached, the conflict between the will of His soul and that of His spirit intensified: "My soul is overwhelmed with sorrow to the point of death," "...The spirit is truly ready, but the flesh is weak."[73] Taking the place of His predecessor, the first Adam, and all of Adam's fallen progeny, was so utterly repulsive to His righteous soul that He sought relief from the shame of it. His spirit, however, retained its unwavering commitment to His destiny, which had been decreed "from the foundation of the world."[74]

The clarity of Jesus' choice to subject His soul to the rule of His spirit, and so return man to an unfallen state, was expressed in His prayer in the garden of Gethsemane on the very night he was betrayed by one of His twelve disciples. He prayed, "Now my soul is troubled, and what shall I say? 'Father, save me from this hour'? No, it was for this very reason I came to this hour. Father, glorify your name!"[75] In that moment, the decline of human culture was arrested; the dominance of the soul over the spirit that began with Adam and continued until then was fully arrested and reversed.

Although the imperatives of provision and protection would continue to govern the majority of human beings, and the orphan culture would continue on until it reaches its apogee, Jesus made man's original culture fully available in the earth as a clear and distinct alternative. It was not, in fact, a new culture but was a reconnection to, and continuance of, the original culture of the sons of God. From this time onward, this culture would advance along a parallel line to the fallen culture, and eventually it would also reach its quintessential expression.

As both cultures continue their development, their divergence is embodied in two distinct expressions. The culture formed out of the soul's perspective of reality would continue along the path of jealousy, envy, and strife, as those who trust in it seek to find well-being through the pursuit of provision and protection. The culture of the spirit will develop into a corporate expression of the full nature of God. Those who choose the latter as their way of life will put on display the love of God. A vital prerequisite to making the choice to live in either the culture of the soul or the spirit is to understand what each is, and how they function.

THE SOUL AND THE SPIRIT

Both the soul and the spirit are similar in their constituent parts. Each has three components, a mind, a will, and a heart. These components serve similar functions within both the soul and the spirit.

The mind serves as the basis for information upon which the spirit or soul bases its view of reality. The will assembles the resources available to the spirit or soul to interact with creation and actualize that reality. The heart supplies the motivation for the pursuit of the reality.

Beyond the similarities of form, the functioning of these three components out of the spirit and the soul produces radically different results.

> *For who among men knows the thoughts of a man except the man's spirit within him? In the same way, no one knows the thoughts of God except the Spirit of God. We have not received the spirit of the world, but the Spirit who is from God, that we may understand what God has freely given to us. This is what we speak, not in the words taught us by human wisdom but in words taught by the Spirit, express-ing spiritual truths in spiritual words. The man without the Spirit does not accept the things that come from the Spirit of God, for they are foolishness to him, and he cannot understand them, because they are spiritually discerned.*[76]

The mind of the soul receives its information from three sources: the world, the flesh, and the devil. "This wisdom descen-deth not from above, but is earthly, sensual, devilish."[77] The world, the flesh, and the demonic appeal directly to man's soul and come from sources that are subject to the control of the enemy. Eve saw that the fruit on the tree was pleasing to the eye, and she had the desire to possess the wisdom that it promised. The information regarding the possibility of hidden wisdom was supplied from the devil, whose motivation was to seduce man from reliance upon the reality supplied by the wisdom of God. These three sources of information were the world, the flesh, and the devil.

When the soul rules, the person is drawn to these sources of information regarding reality. These influences are corrupt. Therefore, the information assembled by the mind of the soul is corrupt, and the resulting conclusions about reality reflect the taint of that corruption.

This is an unreliable view of reality. Reliance upon information assembled by the mind of the soul deceived man into thinking that he was flesh, and naked, prompting him to clothe himself. In his effort, he utilized what skills he had and what resources were available to him, as an exercise of his will in adopting the reality that he now embraced for himself. In addition to clothing himself, in his new view of reality, he felt endangered, and so he hid.

When man hid from God, the heart supplied the requisite emotion that motivated him to undertake these actions—fear. He confessed that he was afraid.[78] Historically, man has believed that the heart was the center of the human being, and although the Scriptures do not refer to the term "emotion," the heart has always been considered the seat of all emotions. Every decision the human makes is based upon an emotion. However, it is common practice to justify decisions to others by the use of reason. In this manner, the heart of the soul often drives the rationale for one's decisions or actions, disconnected from the truth of the circumstances.

Unlike the soul, whose components function independent of God, the components of the spirit are designed to function only in harmony with the Spirit of God. The human spirit remains submerged and inactive until the Spirit of God energizes it. Scripture describes that occurrence as being born again of the Spirit.[79] This act of being born of the Spirit of God awakens the human spirit and begins to reform the human being by restoring the spirit's dominance over man's soul.[80]

Soul Versus Spirit

Since the soul's dominance has been a matter of long standing, supported by an inherited culture over a long period of time, the restoration of the culture of the spirit is progressive, not instantaneous. It begins with the mind of the spirit being instructed by the Spirit of God.

The source of the information on which the mind of the human spirit relies for its view of reality is the Spirit of God. When the wisdom of God informs man's view of reality, man begins to see and understand all things in the same way that God views reality. Man is returned to a heavenly point of view. As we shall see, the Holy Spirit's conviction is stronger than the soul's, and when the human yields to the point of view of his spirit, he begins to take on the mind of Christ. The continuous yielding to this different reality will, over time, effectively renew the mind of the soul.

The will that is employed in the furtherance of a heavenly view of reality must also be supplied by God who wills and does His own pleasure. The Holy Spirit supplies the power that enables the human to function in a heavenly view of reality in the form of "Gifts of the Spirit."[81]

The dominant expression that arises out of the heart that lies within the spirit, and is the motivation of all actions reflecting the activities of the spirit, is love. Love is the only emotion greater than fear. God's perfect love casts out fear.[82] When God designed man, He placed the greatest emotion of which He is capable within man's spirit, thereby assuring that the spirit is always ultimately capable of ruling the human being. Because it is true that whoever loves is born of God, it is always possible for any human being, no matter how depraved, to choose to be born again of God's Spirit. The love of God demonstrated to even the most hardened of human beings has the innate capacity of activating the emotion of love that lies dormant within the heart of his spirit. It is, therefore, the goodness of God that draws men to repentance.[83]

CHAPTER 7

The Schemes
of the Enemy

Put on the full armor of God so that you can take your stand
against the devil's schemes. For our struggle is not against
flesh and blood, but against the rulers, against the authori-
ties, against the powers of this dark world and against the
spiritual forces of evil in the heavenly realms.[84]

From the initial deception of man, Satan proceeded to craft an alternative to God built upon the motivation of fear that lies within the heart of the soul. This entrapment comprises many systems designed to exploit man's fear of death and his obsession with comfort.[85] Though he continues to utilize his minions to harass and exploit people on an individual basis, the greater threat posed by his administration is systemic. These compounded systems make up his alternative kingdom, which is designed to deceive man and to darken his understanding of God, while promising enlightenment of the self. The Scriptures refer to these systems collectively as "the world."

These systems that oppose God and the truth operate on the same basis of Satan's original engagement of man. His schemes are built on the anticipation that man will be governed by his soul. He continues to offer man the opportunity to create and control his own reality. Anyone who relies on these systems pursues the illusion of control, and whether he is aware of it or not, becomes his own god. Because the enemy's schemes appeal to man's soul, these systems have little ability to affect one who is ruled by his spirit. They are ineffective in predicting or controlling the mind of the spirit.

Adam lost his connection to God, changing his perception of himself from spirit to flesh, and began to depend upon the ingenuity of his soul for survival. "The god of this age has blinded the minds of unbelievers, so that they cannot see the light of the gospel of the glory of Christ, who is the image of God."[86] When Adam began to operate out of his soul, he became vulnerable to the schemes of the enemy. Satan fashioned the systems of the world as an entrapment to exploit Adam's separation from the Father.

THE KOSMOS

The Greek term for the compounded systems, known as the world, is *kosmos*.[87] As is common in any language, words in Scripture may have multiple meanings, and the meaning is derived from the context of the surrounding text. There are multiple meanings to the term "world" or "kosmos." The apostle John uses at least two of these meanings. While proclaiming God's love for humans, he declares that "God so loved the world,"[88] but he also cautioned believers in Christ, "Do not love the world" because for anyone who loves the world, "the love of the Father is not in him."[89] The world that John declares God loves is, of course, humanity. The world that he cautions believers against loving or relying upon, the kosmos, has a different creator from God.

When one relies upon the systems of the *kosmos*, he cannot simultaneously trust God, since these systems were created as an alternative to trusting in God, and reliance upon them further separates man from his Father. Therefore, the apostle John admonished:

> *Do not love the world or anything in the world. If anyone*
> *loves the world, the love of the Father is not in him. For*
> *everything in the world—the cravings of sinful man, the lust*

of his eyes and the boasting of what he has and does—comes not from the Father but from the world. The world and its desires pass away, but the man who does the will of God lives forever.[90]

This *kosmos* is based upon the nature of its creator, the one referred to as the *kosmokrator* or world-ruler, an epithet of Satan.[91] It focuses upon man's desire to assure the certainty of his provision and protection. These systems both require and allow one to rely exclusively upon himself, making it impossible to simultaneously rely upon God. The apostle John understood that these systems were designed to seduce anyone who relied upon them away from reliance upon God as their Father. He accurately concluded that one cannot rely on God the Father for provision and protection and simultaneously trust in systems designed to replace a relationship to God with a reliance on one's self.[92]

The strength of Satan's kingdom is the collective appeal of these interconnected systems in that they are designed to address every facet of human life. They represent an orderly arrangement, interwoven like a spider's web, to entrap and to contain the entirety of humanity. Entire nations form their governmental systems to reflect the promise of human capacity inherent in these systems. Even Jesus was tempted to concede the validity and primacy of these systems.[93]

The Systems of the Kosmos

In the earth, all humans belong to one of two kingdoms, either the Kingdom of God or the *kosmos*.[94] The nature of the king over each of these kingdoms defines its citizens' identity. Until we are translated into the Kingdom of God, we are governed by the culture of the orphan, the lasting legacy of our great ancestor Adam, perpetuated by Satan, the god of this world. In the Kingdom of God, however, Christ defines the culture for its citizens. They are sons of God and heirs of the promise of eternal life.

The systems of both kingdoms reflect the nature of their kings.

Eventually, the citizens subject to the respective rulers model the character of the kings, because the culture of the kingdom dictates the characteristics of the citizens' lifestyle. The existence of these different systems is warranted by the need for governmental administrations to address the issues that arise among citizens of any kingdom. The systems of the *kosmos* have their counterparts in the systems of the Kingdom of God, but they radically diverge as they reflect the extreme differences in the natures of their kings.

THE SYSTEM FOR RESOLVING CONFLICTS

Instigating conflict is a classic scheme of the enemy. Therefore, in any kingdom, it is necessary to have in place a system for resolving disputes between its citizens, the goal of which is to determine the relative rights and duties of the parties in conflict and to reach a judgment. The determination of the parties' relative rights and duties centers on that which is deemed valuable within the system.

Value, or the thing to be gained in the resolution of conflict, is determined by the culture of the kingdom. In the *kosmos*, value is measured by the imperatives of provision and protection. In civil disputes, value is assigned to money, property rights, personal property, and intangibles such as health and intellectual property. These are all things to which courts can ascribe monetary value. In criminal matters, the conflict is between the security of the state and its citizens and the liberty interests of an individual.

That which is valuable within the *kosmos* is that over which the state can exercise its authority. Property, money, and one's liberty can be manipulated by the state. Relationships, on the other hand, or those deeper hurts between individuals that take root when one feels wronged, are not the domain of the state, and therefore, they must be set aside when two parties seek to resolve a conflict.

This is an adversarial system that places primary importance on winning, because there is no basis for measuring the value of a relationship between the parties. Any matter submitted for resolution is subject to a process that anticipates each party's zealous advocacy for a one-sided outcome. Although the proceedings may be conducted in an orderly fashion, the parties are more than likely to emerge from the process as adversaries, regardless of which side the result favors. Friends and family members are made enemies simply by submitting a dispute to the authority of the kingdom. This strategy of the dividing of people from each other reflects the nature of the creator of this system who, from the beginning, was successful in severing the relationship between Adam and God.

By contrast, the system for the adjudication of disputes in God's Kingdom starts by affixing value to the relationship between the disputants, making the goal of the process the reconciliation of the parties in dispute. Jesus outlined the steps for reconciliation:

> *If your brother sins against you, go and show him his fault, just between the two of you. If he listens to you, you have won your brother over. But if he will not listen, take one or two others along, so that 'every matter may be established by the testimony of two or three witnesses.' If he refuses to listen to them, tell it to the church; and if he refuses to listen even to the church, treat him as you would a pagan or a tax collector.*[95]

The value of the relationship is preserved throughout the entire process. The initial step of approaching one's brother privately is designed to minimize the potential for his embarrassment and invite reconciliation in an environment of discretion. This approach is conducive to preserving goodwill between the parties, while permitting an honest discussion of the substance of the dispute. Although it is a difficult step to undertake because it requires a face-to-face engagement, it conveys the value that the one who has been wronged places on the relationship with the one who has wronged him. By requiring that the one who was offended initiate the process, it highlights the goal of reconciliation rather than retribution. This matches exactly the attitude of God toward man. For when man sinned against Him, God initiated the process of reconciliation in the person of Jesus Christ.

If the offending party rebuffs the initial attempt at resolution, the process is continued by the inclusion of the least number of people necessary to help bring resolution. These "two or three witnesses" are selected on the basis of their willingness to prefer the reconciliation of the relationship as the primary goal of their inclusion. At the time of Jesus' instruction in this process, "two or three witnesses" was the minimum number necessary to establish a matter by testimony.[96] The term Jesus uses for "witnesses" has a duel meaning. First, it refers to a witness in the legal sense, and second, it describes one who is analogous to a "martyr."[97] In this context, these witnesses are ones who are willing to lay down their lives on behalf of the disputants to achieve a reconciliation of the relationship. Because of the witnesses' devotion to the parties in conflict, these witnesses can be trusted to give an accurate and unbiased assessment of the facts. They are, therefore, in the best position to appeal to the ones in conflict with each other to be reconciled.

If the attempt at reconciliation at this step fails, the witnesses' report of the facts to the spiritual household of the parties precludes the need for a new investigation into the facts. This permits anyone with a relationship to the party at fault to attempt to persuade him to change and be reconciled.

The final step in this process is taken after all the preceding efforts have been exhausted. When the offending party refuses to value the relationship above all else, he is denied the fellowship of the believers on two bases. First, he has consistently devalued his relationship to his brother, showing that he does not have the value system of the King over this culture. Second, he has rejected the council of Christ offered to him throughout the entire process.

In this case, his refusal to submit to the reconciliation offered in the process places him outside the authority of the Kingdom. One in the Kingdom must be submitted to Christ the King. It is that submission that enables the reconciliation of the relationship. The mandate of Christ, rather than forcible control, changes the hearts of people.

If a man rejects the counsel of Christ unwaveringly, he has shown himself not submitted to the Kingdom of God. Before he can be reconciled to his brother, he must be brought within the Kingdom.

The last option for one not submitted is to release him from the protection of the Kingdom and to permit his enemy to rule him through his lusts. Although harsh, this may be the only possibility for bringing him back into the Kingdom. Therefore, even this step is designed to produce the desired result.

Reconciliation pursued in this fashion neither ignores nor minimizes conflict. Instead, it identifies the valuable thing as the relationship, recognizes the existence of the conflict, and moves to establish a factual basis upon which to render a righteous outcome.

This brief comparison highlights the contrast between the two systems arising from the culture of drastically different kingdoms. The goals of both kingdoms are reflected in their respective systems. The identification of the value to be presumed is consistent in each kingdom with the nature and authority of the king. Satan values separation and division, because it furthers his interest in proving God to be wrong in his choice of man as His heir. In contrast, Christ values the reconciliation of the relationship, because He came to restore man to God as sons of God.

KINGDOM AGAINST KINGDOM

The systems of the kosmos are designed around man's desire for provision and protection. The promise of these systems is the illusion of the control over these imperatives. There is a wide array of systems that include education, which is used to glorify the primacy of the intelligence of man; entertainment and culture, which feed his lusts; financial systems and systems of commerce, which supply his provision; and military and political systems, which offer him protection for his person and possessions. Even a religious system will emerge to provide a spiritual legitimacy to all the other systems. These systems, integrated and operating together, will represent the zenith of the culture of the orphan.

Over time, these systems have invaded all aspects of human society. The integration of these systems is producing fewer systems with greater control. As these systems integrate, the result will be a hollowing out of the individual nation's sovereignty, requiring greater loyalties and a global consciousness. Inevitably, the result will be the creation of a sovereign global society, reflecting the mandates of these global systems.

The promise of these systems and their demands will be the basis of a de facto global kingdom. Citizenship in traditional nations will lose all meaningful significance and will retain only symbolic value. In order to comply with the global mandates of this new order of governance, a global citizenry will emerge.

CHAPTER 8

The Last Adam

The conflict between the two kingdoms that embody the ideals surrounding the great conflict between God and Satan, which existed prior to the creation of the world, was inevitable. The earth is the arena in which the conflict is played out and will be finally resolved. In this great drama, man is the principal actor.

In the story of the redemption of man, Christianity has focused nearly exclusively first on the fall of man, then on Christ's death on the cross as the required remedy for man's sin. The importance of the cross in the story of man's redemption is beyond dispute. However, the cross is neither the beginning nor the end of the story.

A focus limited to Christ and the cross does not consider that this event is part of a greater context. That context is a covenant between God the Father and God the Son that preceded creation, which has as its centerpiece the reconciliation of man through Christ. In the context of this precreation covenant, Christ's sacrifice on the cross is the fulcrum upon which the history of man rests and is rectified. Therefore, the relevance of Christ and the cross is best understood within the context of a precreation covenant established between God the Father and God the Son.

Moreover, the existence of this precreation covenant is vital to understanding why God established the creation in the first place.

It also explains why the earth was the designated situs to host the conflict between God and His enemy, Satan, and why man was placed upon the earth in the center of the conflict.

The precreation covenant, rather than chaos, random chance, or even cause-and-effect, governs the course laid out for the creation and for mankind. The unfolding of events within time is carefully calibrated by God to fulfill the requirements of this pre-creation covenant. Human history is not a series of random acts occurring as reactions to conditions existing at particular times in the history of humankind. Instead, it is the seasonal unfolding of things in heaven that were conceived before the creation of the world and destined to appear in time as God had foreordained.

God foreknew that man would sin and planned to rescue him. He laid out the requirements of this plan as essential parts of this precreation—or preexisting—covenant that He obligated Himself to perform. The terms of this covenant include the offer and sat-isfaction of Jesus' death on the cross and God's acceptance of this sacrifice. This covenant is the foundation for the reconciliation of man to God and to the destiny for which God created him.

God established the requirements for the reconciliation of man to His divine purposes before creating him, and God agreed to undertake all that was demanded by these requirements and to perform the requirements Himself. The cross is, therefore, required to rescue man from sin, but it is part of a covenant that is also designed to restore man to the eternal purpose for which man was made.

This is the administration of the mystery of Christ that Paul wrote, "for ages past was kept hidden in God, who created all things."[98] The covenant itself envisioned man being restored to what God made him to be:

> *His intent was that now, through the church, the manifold wisdom of God should be made known to the rulers and authorities in the heavenly realms, according to his eternal purpose that he accomplished in Christ Jesus our Lord. In*

him and through faith in him we may approach God with freedom and confidence.[99]

The greater conflict between God and Satan exists beyond man's reconciliation to God and concerns God's choice of man as His heir. The purpose of Satan's plan to oppose God on all levels of human existence is to discredit humans by attempting to show how unlike God they are. God's answer is to judge Satan, as the father of this great lie, by showing the truth: that man was created to be God's son and heir, that this creation is innately capable of making that choice, and that man is worthy to be called the sons of God and to be appointed the heirs of God.

Beyond the designation as sons of God is the matter of man functioning as sons of God, both in respective individual capacities as well as corporately. Individually, people display the character of God in the way they administrate the authority of God, delegated to them in the form of gifts of the Holy Spirit, and within their personal callings. However, they also are meant to function jointly as a Kingdom. In the larger corporate picture, in the Kingdom of Heaven, they put the righteousness of God on display in contrast to the kingdom of Satan.

The precreation covenant is the skeletal framework that is being filled in with the details God conceived prior to the creation of man. Both God and man participate actively in the fulfillments required by the covenant.

THE OATH AND THE PROMISE

The precreation covenant was established by God's oath to Himself:

Men swear by someone greater than themselves, and the oath confirms what is said and puts an end to all argument. Because God wanted to make the unchanging nature of his purpose very clear to the heirs of what was promised, he confirmed it with an oath. God did this so that, by two un-changeable things in which it is impossible for God to lie, we who have fled to take hold of the hope offered to us may be greatly encouraged. We have this hope as an anchor for the soul, firm and secure. It enters the inner sanctuary behind the curtain, where Jesus, who went before us, has entered on our behalf. He has become a high priest forever, in the order of Melchizedek.[100]

God determined before He made man that He would establish the means by which He could adopt the creation as His sons, knowing man would sin. Therefore, Jesus, the sacrificial Lamb, by whom God swore to save man, was slain from the foundations of the world.[101]

God knew the parameters of man's choice that were necessary, and He knew that man would choose to rebel. Knowing this, God established the means by which man could choose to be fully reconciled to God. The design of man allows him to possess the holy nature of God, by housing God's Spirit, and to rule by choice, so that man could be a son as opposed to another ministering servant. Ideally, man's soul is under the rule of his spirit, and man communes and fellowships with God. But, in order for man to have the ability to choose God, he must also be able to resist God, and even rebel against Him.

Choice would include not only the choice to rebel against God, but also the choice to repent and to be reconciled to God. God would have to provide the means by which this choice was enabled. Once man sinned against God, he would incur a debt that he himself could not pay. God would have to pay on his behalf. The preexisting covenant is the manner in which God established the terms for the reconciliation of man. God swore by himself so that He would be required to pay in full all that was necessary for man to have the ability to choose not only to sin but also to be reconciled to God.

The same God would, therefore, have to become the principal actor on both sides of the covenant. This arrangement is possible for God, since He is Spirit. He may choose to be Himself in infinite representations. For the purposes of this covenant, however, He would choose the manifestations of Father and Son, since these manifestations perfectly captured the existing need. Man would be created as a son of God, and God would take on the role of being his Father. Man could, therefore, understand God Himself appearing as His son to represent the interests of His Father.[102]

Accordingly, God entered into a covenant with Himself, with the Father and the Son as the parties to the covenant—"since there was no one greater for him to swear by, he swore by himself."[103] The Son's part was to take on human form and to come to earth to be the sacrificial Lamb. The Father's part in the covenant was to accept the sacrifice of the Son as a sufficient atonement for all of the sins of all humankind. God would appoint the Son as the mediator of this covenant, thereby giving Him the authority to determine who would benefit from it. The Father and the Son, working in the perfect harmony defined by this covenantal agreement, would neutralize the effects of Adam's actions and nullify all of Satan's activities, which are designed to keep man from his destiny as sons and heirs of God.[104] The precreation covenant would reopen the way to God for man, and man could once again view God as his Father and himself as a viceroy of the Kingdom of Heaven.

FROM SYMBOL TO REALITY

The coming of Jesus as the Son of God to be sacrificed, according to the terms of this covenant, was foreordained, and this foreordination was revealed through Jesus as "the Lamb slain from the foundation of the world." God inserted the knowledge of the existence of this covenant, specifically the requirement of Jesus' sacrifice, into man's culture shortly after the fall of man. This cultural knowledge existed in the form of a lamb's sacrifice.

The exact time of the introduction of this knowledge is not

clear from Scripture. However, Abel understood to offer this sacrifice to God in substitution for his own sin. God showed His pleasure at Abel's sacrifice of a lamb and displeasure at Cain's offering of "fruits of the soil."[105] The lamb became the appropriate and requisite sacrifice to God as a central tenant of the culture that continued to seek Him, because it was the symbol in which the knowledge of the covenant was maintained.

Later, God would test Abraham by asking him to sacrifice Isaac, his son. This was a foreshadowing of the relationship between God and Jesus, and one that advanced the understanding behind the requirement of the sacrifice of a lamb. In the story, God spared Isaac and provided a ram to be sacrificed in his stead. In the fact that God provided the lamb in the story of Abraham and Isaac, the significance of the sacrifice was extended to demonstrate God's promise to be the lamb Himself.

This symbol of the covenant was maintained and expanded during the time of the deliverance of Israel from Egyptian slavery. God passed over Israel while destroying the firstborn of Egyptian households the night before He liberated Israel from Egypt. The death of the Egyptian firstborn is analogous to the condition of death surrounding Adam, the first of God's two sons to be placed in creation. The firstborn of the houses of Israel were spared because the entrances to the houses in which they lived were smeared with the blood of the lamb applied in the form of a cross. The symbol of the lamb would continue to evidence the existence of the covenant, with the Levitical priests annually offering the blood of a lamb on the "Day of Atonement" for the sins of the entire nation of Israel.

God preserved the knowledge of the covenant in the earth so that when the One who was actually the Lamb to be sacrificed was revealed, human culture would have a basis for interpreting the relevance of Jesus on the cross. This was the singular act required in the Son's performance of the covenant that would implicate all the terms of the covenant.

When John the Baptist declared, "Look, the Lamb of God,

who takes away the sin of the world,"[106] he would do so against the background of the traditions of the Levitical order, which was charged with maintaining this symbolic reference to the preexisting, precreation covenant through the law of sacrifice. John himself was a legitimate priest of this order, since priesthood was hereditary and John's father had served in the temple as a priest who officiated in the practice of offering sacrifices. The ritual associated with the offering of sacrificial lambs included the responsibility to examine, select, and designate perfect lambs for sacrifice, and also to wash them prior to sacrificing them. This explains why John identifies Jesus as the reality that had come to fulfill the symbolic representations. Having done so, John, in accordance with the customs of the law regarding the designated sacrifice, baptizes Jesus in anticipation of His crucifixion.

To the culture of the time, John's actions were both legitimate and transformational. The reality of Christ had replaced the symbol of the sacrificial lamb. This key requirement of the precreation covenant was declared to be satisfied.

CHRIST FULFILLS THE COVENANT

Since the precreation covenant is the foundation for the relationship of God and man, God established the covenant to be unimpeachable. He accomplished this with an oath. In ancient times, the strongest support for an oath was the reputation of the person who gave his oath. God clearly intends the same force of affirmation as when Jesus Himself declared, "Heaven and earth will pass away, but my words will never pass away."[107] By committing Himself to an oath, guaranteed by the integrity of His person, God established for all time the reliability and certainty of the precreation covenant. Psalm 138 recognizes the status of the oath sworn by God: "I will bow down toward your holy temple and will praise your name for your unfailing love and your faithfulness, for you have so exalted your solemn decree that it surpasses your fame."[108] Creation itself was established to accommodate the sequential unfolding of the precreation covenant. The fulfillment of this covenant is absolute and inevitable.

The covenant created an estate that is conveyed to man, the intended beneficiaries, by a promise. With respect to the covenant, Jesus represents the interests of man. He is the Mediator between God and man. Since He is God, clothed in the form of man, He is the perfect Mediator. As God, He is fully aware of the mind of God and the interests of God to be satisfied by the covenant. He is righteous, as God is righteous, and cannot compromise God's standards of righteousness, and He fully satisfies all of its requirements. On the other hand, Jesus is the Creator of man. "In the beginning was the Word, and the Word was with God, and the Word was God. He was with God in the beginning. Through him all things were made; without him nothing was made that has been made."[109] He created man to be sons of God. He, therefore, came to display among men the perfect picture of what He designed.

By modeling the perfect design to man, His life illuminates the understanding of who they were made to be. By doing so, He removes the darkness of sin that had clouded man's understanding of his true purpose for being in creation since the fall occurred. "For although they knew God, they neither glorified him as God nor gave thanks to him, but their thinking became futile and their foolish hearts were darkened."[110] By illuminating the darkness, He becomes the "light of the world."[111]

Jesus Himself swore an oath. Jesus has the same standing as God in regard to the precreation covenant, because by its terms an oath makes the parties to it equal. He must fulfill all of its requirements, even though it consumed His life as a man. Jesus accepted the full implications of the covenant the night before He was crucified, saying, "My Father, if it is possible, may this cup be taken from me. Yet not as I will, but as you will."[112] "Because of this oath Jesus has become the guarantee of a better covenant."[113] The Levitical covenant that focused on the sacrifice for atonement foreshadowed the fulfillment of the preexisting covenant. Jesus, however, is the actual sacrifice and accomplishes the atonement. He, therefore, guarantees a better result.

As delegates of the Lord Jesus Christ, sons of God possess His authority to cancel men's debts against God and to invite them to take up citizenship within the Kingdom of Heaven. As ambassadors of the Kingdom of Heaven, they operate under the protections of the authority of the Holy Spirit who equips them with gifts of Jesus' authority commensurate with the spheres of administration to which they are assigned. Like Jesus, their administration reconciles men to God and brings about lasting peace in the lives of people. As the ancient figure Melchizedek, they serve as righteous priests empowered by kingly authority—a royal priesthood.

Jesus, in His life as a man, fully modeled the result of this precreation covenant. His estate possesses all the requisite authority to select sons of God from among the race of humankind and to form them into a royal priesthood that puts on display the nature of God.

> *And they sang a new song, saying:*
> *"You are worthy to take the scroll and to open its seals, because you were slain, and with your blood you purchased for God members of every tribe and language and people and nation. You have made them to be a kingdom and priests to serve our God, and they will reign on the earth."*
>
> *Then I looked and heard the voice of many angels, numbering thousands upon thousands, and ten thousand times ten thousand. They encircled the throne and the living creatures and the elders. In a loud voice they were saying:*
> *"Worthy is the Lamb, who was slain, to receive power and wealth and wisdom and strength and honor and glory and praise!"*[114]

THE TESTAMENT OF THE LORD JESUS CHRIST

> *My prayer is not for them alone. I pray also for those who will believe in me through their message, that all of them may be one, Father, just as you are in me and I am in you. May they*

also be in us so that the world may believe that you have sent me. I have given them the glory that you gave me, that they may be one as we are one.[115]

Jesus gave the content of His estate in the covenant to those who were called and selected to be sons of God. The "New Testament" describes Jesus' estate and its administration and names the inheritors of Jesus' estate as "sons of God" who are drawn from all the nations of humankind. In order to be added to the class of heirs, one must first be rescued from the control of the kosmos and be made a citizen of the Kingdom of Heaven:

[A]nd giving joyful thanks to the Father, who has qualified you to share in the inheritance of his people in the kingdom of light. For he has rescued us from the dominion of darkness and brought us into the kingdom of the Son he loves, in whom we have redemption, the forgiveness of sins.[116]

Those who are already vested heirs are empowered to invite others to become members of the class.[117]

Within the designation "sons of God" exists degrees of maturity and inheritance. Being translated into the Kingdom of God, one is initially and automatically named as an heir of Christ. However, each individual must undergo an extensive process of change and transformation from the culture of orphans to the culture of sons, and subsequently, to the status of mature sons. Only by this process can one faithfully represent the Father in all things. Therefore, in the Scriptures there is a spectrum of sonship related to one's maturity. For example, the word used for one who is "born again" and in the infantile state is *nepios*, of which Paul wrote in his letter to the Galatians, "What I am saying is that as long as the heir is *a child*, he is no different from a slave, although he owns the whole estate."[118] This is distinguished from a *teknon* of which the apostle John wrote, "But as many as received him, to them gave he power to become *the sons* of God...."[119] Here the word used for "sons," *teknon*, implies a son with sufficient maturity to have a reciprocal relationship with a father, defined by love, friendship, and trust; such as a disciple.[120]

Similarly, in his letter to the Romans, Paul wrote that "those who are led by the Spirit of God are sons of God," referring to a son in the *huios* stage, which is one who is a mature son, fit to represent the Father.[121] As sons grow in maturity, the Holy Spirit endows them with greater measures of their inheritance. The scope of their representation of God the Father is widened accordingly, and the power that sustains them is increased accordingly.

The Holy Spirit, whom Jesus specifically commissioned to represent Him, faithfully executes the terms of inheriting His estate.

> *But very truly I tell you, it is for your good that I am going away. Unless I go away, the Advocate will not come to you; but if I go, I will send him to you.*
>
> *…I have much more to say to you, more than you can now bear. But when he, the Spirit of truth, comes, he will guide you into all the truth. He will not speak on his own; he will speak only what he hears, and he will tell you what is yet to come. He will glorify me because it is from me that he will receive what he will make known to you. All that belongs to the Father is mine. That is why I said the Spirit will receive from me what he will make known to you.* [122]

Jesus described the Holy Spirit as the Spirit of the Father, whose work Jesus had come to do, and from whom Jesus inherited that part of the estate that originally belonged to the Father. The Holy Spirit is Himself God, just as are Jesus and the Father. The Spirit is intimately familiar with everything Jesus sought to present in His life on the earth. He is capable of directing the process of the selection of sons through the ambassadors, and He distributes gifts of the authority of Jesus commensurate with the standards of maturity to which sons matriculate. He is, therefore, the perfect Executor. That is why Jesus has committed into His administration the sole, absolute, and exclusive representation of His interests in the earth.

Any administration of the estate of the Lord Jesus Christ that takes place outside of this basis of authority is categorically illegitimate, is an invalid administration, and is empty of power. The administration of the estate of the Lord Jesus Christ has not been left subject to the collective will of the heirs. All delegates of the Kingdom of God purporting to act on behalf of the Lord Jesus Christ must derive their authority to do so from the Holy Spirit Himself. Every action undertaken apart from this specific protocol is exercised in opposition to the administration set by the Lord Jesus Himself.

Such alternative administrations are actively opposed to Christ's interests.[123] The Holy Spirit is the active agent for the administration of Jesus' estate. He chooses to work through those who are already sons of God to bring others into the Kingdom. However, no one is empowered to act in furtherance of the administration of the Lord's estate independent of the Holy Spirit. The Holy Spirit remains in total control of all facets of the administration of the estate of Jesus Christ.

COVENANT AND PROMISE

Brothers and sisters, let me take an example from everyday life. Just as no one can set aside or add to a human covenant that has been duly established, so it is in this case. The promises were spoken to Abraham and to his seed. Scripture does not say "and to seeds," meaning many people, but "and to your seed," meaning one person, who is Christ. What I mean is this: The law, introduced 430 years later, does not set aside the covenant previously established by God and thus do away with the promise. For if the inheritance depends on the law, then it no longer depends on the promise; but God in his grace gave it to Abraham through a promise.[124]

82

Covenant and promise—these two terms have particular, distinct meanings, though they are commonly confused and frequently used interchangeably. The *covenant* is the precreation covenant between God the Father and the Son before the establishment of creation itself. This agreement between God and God formed the basis for the structure and operation of all creation that followed. The requirements of this covenant foreordained the trajectory of human history. This covenant produced an estate to both the Father and the Son, with the intention that the contents of this estate be conveyed to man. God entered into this covenant with the intention of benefiting man prior to his existence, in anticipation of his creation. The benefits to man were held in trust by a promise.

The *promise* would vest when the intended heirs arrived. So, when God created Adam, his status was that of both a son and an heir. As the first son of God, the benefits of the covenant vested with him. However, when he sided with the enemy of God, he rejected his estate as a son, choosing independence from God instead. The estate remained, however, since its existence depends on God's oath and is, therefore, immutable. In essence, with Adam's rejection, the estate reconverted to a promise, once again awaiting an heir.

God found an heir in Abraham and gave him as much of the promise as Abraham's condition would allow him to receive—although Abraham acted out of a heart that desired God, as a son of Adam his culture was already compromised. God promised to make a great nation out of Abraham and to bring through his line Christ the Son, by whom all of the incidences of the estate would vest. By selecting Abraham to be the father of the race out of whom Jesus would come, God initiated the process by which the promise would eventually vest.

When Christ came as both the Son of God and of Abraham, he was positioned to fulfill the remaining requirements of the covenant and to cause the promise to fully vest. Upon His death and resurrection, the promise moved from the realm of hope and expectation to reality, and the estate was fully gathered up and ready to be distributed.

The intent of God that was the subject of the precreation covenant had transitioned fully from covenant to reality. The sons of God assembled to Christ are the reality envisioned by the covenant. By this assembling, the House of God is present and functioning in the earth.

> *So in Christ Jesus you are all children of God through faith, for all of you who were baptized into Christ have clothed yourselves with Christ. There is neither Jew nor Gentile, neither slave nor free, neither male nor female, for you are all one in Christ Jesus. If you belong to Christ, then you are Abraham's seed, and heirs according to the promise.*[125]

THE MAN FROM HEAVEN

The first son, Adam, brought separation from God and alienated man from his Father. By his actions, the House of God fell into disrepute.

From the creation of the world, God promised the restoration of His House through another Son, who would remain faithful to the mandates of His heavenly origin. He would be called "the Last Adam."

> *So it is written: "The first man Adam became a living being"; the last Adam, a life-giving spirit. The spiritual did not come first, but the natural, and after that the spiritual. The first man was of the dust of the earth; the second man is of heaven. As was the earthly man, so are those who are of the earth; and as is the heavenly man, so also are those who are of heaven. And just as we have borne the image of the earthly man, so shall we bear the image of the heavenly man.*[126]

Everyone who lives on the earth is born from Adam, the first son, and has, as his default culture, the mindset of the orphan. With the coming of the last Adam, it is also possible to be born again of this

Son of God. He is given the title "the Christ" to signify that He exists to fulfill God's intention to have sons. When Jesus, the last Adam, completed the requirements of the precreation covenant and the promises vested in Him, the restoration of man to the original purpose of God as foreordained through the preexisting covenant could proceed. Once again, man could become sons of God through Christ Jesus.

All who are to be sons of God necessarily have a second birth experience. This experience is the activation of the spirit within a person and the restoration of the rule of his spirit over his soul. This results in a different order of governance within the person's being. Such a person experiences a change in the mind that governs him, from the mind of the soul to the mind of the spirit, and becomes a person of the spirit. Therefore, Jesus said, "Flesh gives birth to flesh, but the Spirit gives birth to spirit. You should not be surprised at my saying, 'You must be born again.'"[127] Similarly, the apostle Paul writes, "Do not conform to the pattern of this world, but be transformed by the renewing of your mind. Then you will be able to test and approve what God's will is—his good, pleasing and perfect will."[128]

Although the last Adam appeared in the person of Jesus, ultimately what He came to accomplish was to create a spiritual reality to which others could be assembled. The first Adam had heirs who came out of his physical being. The last Adam presents sons to God who are heirs of God's estate through Christ's spiritual being. The body of Adam, from which all men have come, is a natural body. It is not possible to have a relationship with the man Jesus, because no one is added to his physical being, nor does anyone come out of his natural form. The body of Christ is a spiritual body to which the Holy Spirit assembles all who are the sons of God.

When one is born again, he experiences the reemergence of his spirit to the place of preeminence within his being, and he is suitable to be assembled as a spirit into the corporate Christ.

Just as a body, though one, has many parts, but all its many parts form one body, so it is with Christ. For we were all baptized by one Spirit so as to form one body—whether Jews or Gentiles, slave or free—and we were all given the one Spirit to drink. ...Now you are the body of Christ, and each one of you is a part of it.[129]

A spiritual being, assembled to the Body of Christ, is no longer subject to the factors that govern the natural man.

Praise be to the God and Father of our Lord Jesus Christ, who has blessed us in the heavenly realms with every spiritual blessing in Christ. For he chose us in him before the creation of the world to be holy and blameless in his sight. In love he predestined us for adoption to sonship through Jesus Christ, in accordance with his pleasure and will—to the praise of his glorious grace, which he has freely given us in the One he loves. In him we have redemption through his blood, the forgiveness of sins, in accordance with the riches of God's grace that he lavished on us. With all wisdom and understanding, he made known to us the mystery of his will according to his good pleasure, which he purposed in Christ, to be put into effect when the times reach their fulfillment—to bring unity to all things in heaven and on earth under Christ.[130]

In Him we were also chosen, having been predestined according to the plan of Him who works out everything in conformity with the purpose of His will, in order that we, who were the first to put our hope in Christ, might be for the praise of His glory. And you also were included in Christ when you heard the message of truth, the gospel of your salvation. When you believed, you were marked in Him with a seal, the promised Holy Spirit, who is a deposit guaranteeing our inheritance until the redemption of those who are God's possession—to the praise of His glory.[131]

86

The intention of God, as specified in the precreation covenant, is to grant to humans access into the estate created by the covenant through a spiritual union with Christ. His specific intent was to restore the primacy of the spirit of man within his being and to assemble the man, so arranged, into the spiritual entity described as the Christ, of which body the Lord Jesus is the head and rules the body on the earth from His seat on the throne of God in heaven. He effectuates this rule through the agency of the Holy Spirit, who in turn prosecutes the interests of Christ through the members of the Body of Christ. Sons of God are, therefore, inherently parts of the Body of Christ. This is the manner in which access into the estate of Jesus is secured.

By raising Jesus from the dead, God confirmed that He was the Christ.[132] This was the essential message that was proclaimed on the Day of Pentecost when the gospel of Jesus Christ was first declared on the earth, together with the invitation to depart from the deception of the kosmos and to find refuge under the rule of the ascended King.

Salvation has never been, therefore, just a matter of going to heaven, but is the process by which man is saved from the condition of separation from God that has existed since the days of the first Adam. Once saved from the culture of self-reliance, one is assembled into the spiritual man and reunited with his true purpose for being. In the Body of Christ, the Holy Spirit is available to empower one's calling. Although salvation includes avoiding the annihilation of hell, that result is neither the focus of the gospel of Jesus Christ nor its primary result. When a person is joined to Christ, he is no longer subject to the law of sin and death.[133] That is an existing state of being, the guarantee of which is the seal of the Holy Spirit.[134]

The overarching purpose of salvation is to reacquaint us with the purposes for which we were originally created. This is accomplished primarily by the removal of the mindset inherited from the first Adam, our natural father, and the reorientation by the Holy Spirit to the purposes of God, consistent with being His heirs. Salvation means being saved from the mindset and culture of an orphan and reintegrated into the House of God, by which process we are renewed as His sons. "To be carnally minded is death, but to be spiritually minded is life and peace."[135] The life of a son is lived in deep fellowship with the Holy Spirit as part of the corporate Christ.

CHAPTER 9

How God Speaks

Even though man has been restored to his position as God's son, he retains the culture of the orphan, and it determines how he relates to God. The culture of the orphan filters the sound of the voice of God. It muffles God's voice to one's spirit, such that even a born-again believer will begin to accept the assumption that it is impossible to hear God directly, a view generally propagated by religious institutions.

Prior to the fall, God spoke to man face to face in the Garden. Since man is spirit, such communication was neither strange nor difficult for man. However, since the fall, the clarity of God's communication with man has been distorted by the preeminence of the soul's mind. In spirit, man is of the same kind and nature as God, because the spirit of man came out of the person of God. Man was not preoccupied originally with either his provision or his protection, since the true nature of man's being is spirit. His communication with God was not distracted by his preoccupation with these imperatives.

God spoke to man to inform him and equip him to fulfill his commission as the representation of God in the earth. Man's rule was to reflect the character of God. There was harmony between God and man, and the resulting communication was flawless. This was the original way in which God intended to communicate with His sons.

Jesus communicated with God in this fashion while He was on the earth. His intimate familiarity with God was one of the greatest offenses to the people of His day. It was "for this reason they tried all the more to kill him; not only was he breaking the Sabbath, but he was even calling God his own Father, making himself equal with God."[136] Jesus explained:

> *Very truly I tell you, the Son can do nothing by himself; he can do only what he sees his Father doing, because whatever the Father does the Son also does. For the Father loves the Son and shows him all he does. Yes, and he will show him even greater works than these, so that you will be amazed.*[137]

According to Jesus, God chose this method of direct communication. In the beginning, God spoke with Adam face to face, and when God began to restore man, He also spoke face to face with Jesus.

Since the time of Adam, before the advent of Jesus, God continually attempted to speak face to face with man but had very limited success. He spoke to Moses out of the burning bush, but when He attempted to speak to all Israel on Mount Sinai, they ran from His presence. In their fallen state, like that of Adam, they confessed to being afraid of the presence of God. Moses recounted the event in Deuteronomy, saying, "The LORD spoke to you face to face out of the fire on the mountain. (At that time I stood between the LORD and you to declare to you the word of the LORD, because you were afraid of the fire and did not go up the mountain.)"[138]

At times, various groups or individuals have suggested that it is the height of arrogance and presumption to suggest that an individual can actually hear God. In particular, those steeped in the culture of religion often attribute an attitude of pride and hubris to those who claim to hear God. Though it is true that often people claiming to hear from God attribute things to God that are clearly inconsistent with either the Scriptures or the Holy Spirit, the heart of the resistance to the idea that a person may hear directly from God is a lack of expectation. The culture of the orphan has no capacity for the intimacy with the Father that would cause the Father to earnestly desire direct communication with the spirit of His son.

FACE TO FACE

When a person refuses to believe that God would choose to speak face to face with a son, he has failed to recognize the distinction between flesh and spirit, by continuing to see man as flesh. Man as merely flesh provides no framework for understanding communication that takes place between the Spirit of God and the spirit of man. Yet, the stubborn refusal to acknowledge that it is in fact the desire of God to speak directly often is disguised by false modesty, presented as humility.

Scripture shows a picture of God continuously seeking communication with man throughout all the epochs of history. The assertion that a holy God would never deign to speak directly to a sinful man, and for man to claim such familiarity with God is close to blasphemy, has deeper roots in Gnosticism than Scripture. From before the creation of the world, God knew that when man sinned God would have to speak to him differently. So, He planned how He would communicate with man once He could no longer speak to him face to face.

When man sinned, the preeminence of his soul provided him with a different, misinformed view of reality. This reality provided no basis for man's harmonious interaction with God and creation. Yet, the precreation covenant committed God to the establishment of a holy nation, drawn from all the races of humankind and remained as the irrevocable guideline for the evolution of human history. So, God included in His plan for creation the ways by which creation speaks to man's soul. He established creation to be a continual source of information, designed to remind man of God's intentions.

Although the culture of the orphan continued to widen

the gulf between man and God, the planned order of creation, together with various other symbolic observations and practices associated with religion, continued to affect human culture with the knowledge of God. "For since the creation of the world God's invisible qualities—His eternal power and divine nature—have been clearly seen, being understood from what has been made, so that people are without excuse."[139] These influences are veiled as shadowy images that reference realities that lay beyond the ability of the soul to grasp, but come into view when the spirit of man parts the veil of his soul, and man may once again see all things through the eyes of his spirit.

Prior to the restoration of man to God, God expected only such responses from man as the unenlightened soul is capable of producing. God did not refrain from pursuing His purposes in the earth. Rather, He pursued those ends with the awareness that man's soul cannot grasp His true intent. God knew that when He communicated to man through natural, as opposed to spiritual, means, man could understand the symbols, types, shadows, and analogies present in creation, but he could not see the purpose or intent behind them. In this state, man could only see the things of God as in a mirror dimly.[140] Therefore, when God spoke to man concerning the principle of the innocent atoning for the sins of those who are guilty, He did so by establishing the sacrifice of a lamb in man's culture; and God fed Israel for forty years with manna, when His true intent was to prepare them for "the bread of life" from heaven, Jesus.[141]

God could not speak about the future plainly, because men could not receive the information with their spirits. Instead, God spoke to man through prophetic utterances, often in the form of visions and dreams, and would wink at man's uninformed views and responses until the restoration of God's communion with man's spirit. God's purpose for establishing symbols, shadows, and types, between the fall and the restoration, was to maintain a connection between man's culture on the earth and the culture of heaven, in anticipation of the day when the divine order of heaven would again be restored to the earth.

To understand how God speaks to man, it is necessary to recognize that reality exists simultaneously on the planes of the natural and the spiritual. The soul sees all things exclusively from a natural perspective. "The man without the Spirit does not accept the things that come from the Spirit of God, for they are foolishness to him, and he cannot understand them, because they are spiritually discerned."[142] The soul's mind lacks the capacity to understand the subtleties and the multidimensional platforms of spiritual realities, whereas the spirit apprehends spiritual realities as they exist in heaven and are manifested in the natural creation. Since God speaks to the souls of men through natural images, He may preserve a predisposition toward the truth until the Holy Spirit reveals God's mind. The Holy Spirit reveals the true meanings of what had been previously cloaked in types and shadows to the spirit of man.

The soul continues to wrestle with the spirit for control of the human being; and though it is always possible to make choices by the spirit, man, in his immaturity, will often default to the vision of reality with which his soul has become familiar over the years of his life. "Those who live according to the flesh have their minds set on what that nature desires; but those who live in accordance with the Spirit have their minds set on what the Spirit desires."[143]

GOD KNOWS THE END FROM THE BEGINNING

Since God knows the end of every matter, He was able to structure the early stages of His relationship with man in a fashion that predisposes man to understand his true intentions as they are revealed in succeeding epochs. In this structure, God's dealings with man appear as cyclical occurrences, where recurring themes take on greater depth and profundity as the cycles reoccur.

This approach benefits man by giving him a historical point of reference against which he may understand present occurrences. When these cycles reoccur more than twice, in ever widening scopes that include greater details, they predispose the spirit of man to an anticipation of what the future entails. When man views these cycles through his soul, they remain curious coincidences with little indications of mysteries being revealed. However, when viewed through his spirit, they create an expectation that becomes the foundation of faith, "the substance of things hoped for, the evidence of things not seen."[144]

Jesus is presented in the Gospel of John as the person of the Godhead who designed the creation. "In the beginning was the Word, and the Word was with God, and the Word was God. He was with God in the beginning. …He came to that which was his own, but his own did not receive him."[145] He created the world and humankind knowing exactly what the end would be like before He issued the first edicts of creation. The created world was the last piece of the puzzle to be put in place as the stage upon which the drama of man fulfilling an eternal purpose would unfold. He designed the creation to accommodate the precise unfolding of divine intentions. Once creation was complete, God entered into His rest, knowing the certainty of the outcome.

The spiritual man is invited to enter God's rest and enjoy the peace that comes from knowing the totality of God's control over the unfolding of human events.

> [W]e speak of God's secret wisdom, a wisdom that has been hidden and that God destined for our glory before time began. None of the rulers of this age understood it, for if they had, they would not have crucified the Lord of glory.[146]
>
> Things beyond our seeing, things beyond our hearing, things beyond our imagining, all prepared by God for those who love him, these it is that God has revealed to us through the Spirit.[147]

Communicating the mysteries of heaven to man, God introduced themes early in the history of man that He has developed as time has advanced. Therefore, Jesus, the Lamb of God, was both slain from the foundation of the world and, through the cycles of time, sacrificed at Calvary. In the intervening time, God spoke to man about this eventuality through natural practices. As a result, there are numerous instances throughout the Scriptures in which lambs are slain as atonement for sins. Each succeeding cycle of this tenet that is present in Scripture contains greater meaning and adds depth to the symbol right up until John the Baptist announced that Jesus was the reality—"the Lamb of God, who takes away the sin of the world"—who gave full expression to all that had been symbolically preserved in the culture.

Similarly, all the great themes of human history—such as father and son, birth, death and resurrection, atonement, and faith and love—are both cyclical and concurrent. The types and shadows of these cycles recur, coming closer together until they actually overlay each other at the point where the shadows merge into the spiritual reality. One's understanding of the reality referenced by the cycles and the veiled truths they contain grows commensurate with his maturity.

The more mature one becomes, the greater the wisdom and insight that is imparted to him by the Spirit of God. The process of maturing is designed to limit and restrict the input of the soul in determining the nature of reality. The soul's determination to remain in control is the principle inhibitor, limiting the human's ability to grasp reality as revealed from God's point of view.

This process is inseparable from suffering and the apparent loss of control. Suffering is experienced when the soul perceives that its view of reality is shifting from a basis of reason to one of revelation. The soul may control the process of reason and the decisions that come from it, but it is incapable of influencing the substance of revelation. The corresponding vulnerability makes the human feel adrift and at the mercy of the unknown. This loss of control is one of the human's greatest fears, but it is necessary to allow one's spirit to part the veil of the apparent loss of control and return to the reality of the spirit and the provision and protection of the Kingdom of God.

God sees the end and the beginning in an instant and unifies all the themes in every epoch in such a fashion that the end of the age is the climactic summation of all the themes converging into a single reality:

> *[H]e made known to us the mystery of his will according to his good pleasure, which he purposed in Christ, to be put into effect when the times reach their fulfillment—to bring unity to all things in heaven and on earth under Christ.*
>
> *In him we were also chosen, having been predestined according to the plan of him who works out everything in conformity with the purpose of his will, in order that we, who were the first to put our hope in Christ, might be for the praise of his glory.*[148]

CREATION AS A TYPE AND SHADOW

The gap between God and man widened following the fall; and with the passing of long centuries, the task of restoring man to the original intent of God became formidable. God destined the human race to come from the first man and woman He created. Consequently, the generations of man inherited the orphan culture of their forebears. However, God continued to speak to man through natural and physical means, with the cumulative effect of preparing the world for the coming of Christ and the repositioning of man as sons of God. The work of restoring the fatherhood of God through Christ was placed upon this foundation. This work will culminate at the end of the age with the full revelation of Christ through His spiritual body.

God began creation by arranging preexisting elements. "Now the earth was formless and empty, darkness was over the surface of the deep, and the Spirit of God was hovering over the waters."[149] Prior to God's first act of creation recorded in Scripture, some of the things that already existed were "the deep,"[150] "the waters,"[151] and the land covered by the waters.[152] Prior to God speaking the words that would form the present creation, the deep, the waters, and the earth were not arranged in their present form. He com-

96

manded the dry land to appear and separated the waters with a firmament. He removed the darkness upon the surface of the deep by commanding light to appear, and He gathered the waters below the firmament into a continuous body of water, permitting the dry land underneath to appear.

God arranged the preexisting elements purposefully to accommodate the existence of man. (After the first four days of reorganizing the existing elements, He then begins to call forth acts of pure creation.) This manner of beginning a new creation, by reordering elements that already exist, is the same process by which God creates a son out of one whose life has become formless and misdirected without the preeminence of His spirit.

The functioning of the Godhead in creating the natural world was such that the Holy Spirit was hovering over the elements as they existed, awaiting the commands for creation to issue from the throne of God. Jesus, previously known as "the Word [who] became flesh," issued the commands.[153] The Holy Spirit executed them. And, the result was the present order of arrangement. This method of creating is a type and shadow preceding the recreation of the fallen man into sons of God.

The resulting new creation begins with a rearrangement of the existing order. "[I]f anyone is in Christ, the new creation has come: The old has gone, the new is here!"[154] This "new creation" is in contrast to one's existence being perceived according to his fleshly or worldly nature, "So from now on we regard no one from a worldly point of view."[155] The control of the soul over the spirit is undone, and the soul is placed again under the rule of the spirit. As a result, the body is liberated from its use to accommodate the sinful desires of man and becomes available to the spirit to put on display the glory of God. The Holy Spirit accomplishes the separation and rearrangement of these fundamental elements of the human being into their proper order.

As in the first creation described in Genesis 1, Jesus is seated on the throne of God in heaven, and the Holy Spirit has been positioned to execute His commands in the being of each person in whom Christ is formed.[156] The Holy Spirit begins by rearranging the order of spirit, soul, and body to the original intent of God.

The Holy Spirit is present in each believer, waiting to execute the commands of Christ regarding that particular person. The Holy Spirit empowers a person's belief in Christ and transforms human nature into a divine nature. He constructs faith out of unformed convictions and brings the light of revelation to separate us from the darkness of unbelief. The divine nature of God replaces human nature and evinces the process at work in which Christ is being formed in the person.

The events of one's early years as a believer typically elicit this massive reformatting of the person's nature. Often, one will undergo a period of suffering and an apparent loss of control. The soul is addicted to control which is, at best, an illusion of reality, because one is never actually in control. The antidote to control is faith. Suffering and trials disabuse the soul of its notions of sovereign preeminence by exposing the weaknesses and limitations inherent in the soul. One cannot put on display the character of Christ in any area in which the person's soul retains its preeminence. As the dominance of the spirit is restored, the divine nature into which one is born again begins to emerge preeminently.

GOD SPEAKS THROUGH TYPES AND SHADOWS

God always intended two creations. The natural creation came first to prepare the way and give insight into the process of the spiritual reconstruction. Everything in the natural world has its counterpart in the spiritual realm. The Spirit provides clarity by lifting the veil that would limit one's perception of reality to merely the natural world:

> *And even if our gospel is veiled, it is veiled to those who are perishing. The god of this age has blinded the minds of unbelievers, so that they cannot see the light of the gospel that displays the glory of Christ, who is the image of God. For what we preach is not ourselves, but Jesus Christ as Lord, and ourselves*

as your servants for Jesus' sake. For God, who said, "Let light
shine out of darkness," made his light shine in our hearts to
give us the light of the knowledge of God's glory displayed in
the face of Christ.[157]

The glory of an eternal perspective dimmed as man's soul interfered with his communion with God Spirit to spirit, and the realities of this perspective appeared only as shadows upon a veil. As long as the veil remained, the truth existed just outside of the reach of man's reason.

Even this theme of a veil between God and man is presented in type and shadow in Scripture when the nation of Israel stood at the base of Mount Sinai forty days after their release from slavery in Egypt. God invited them to come up into His presence and to meet with Him face to face. Their souls were overcome with paralyzing fear, and they rejected the invitation, choosing instead to send Moses as their representative. As a result of his encounter with God, Moses' face became so radiant after being in the presence of God that it was necessary for him to wear a veil for some time afterward, until the glory faded. By this, God was showing that in their choice of an intermediary between themselves and God, they had voluntarily placed a barrier between themselves and God. This barrier was an alternative that accommodated the continued rule of the soul. The form of this barrier was reflected in the giving of the law, because the law was a shadow of the good things to come.[158]

In his letter to the Corinthians, Paul used this type to teach about the relationship between types and shadows and the corresponding spiritual reality:

Now if the ministry that brought death, which was engraved
in letters on stone, came with glory, so that the Israelites could
not look steadily at the face of Moses because of its glory,
transitory though it was, will not the ministry of the Spirit
be even more glorious? If the ministry that brought condem-

nation was glorious, how much more glorious is the ministry that brings righteousness! For what was glorious has no glory now in comparison with the surpassing glory. And if what was transitory came with glory, how much greater is the glory of that which lasts![59]

Fundamental to one's understanding of how God speaks to man through types and shadows is that the glory of the spiritual reality far supersedes that of the veiled natural representation.

Since the true intent of God is to create the natural to reflect the spiritual, only when the spiritual reality appears can the natural be properly understood. Religious practice is based largely upon relating to the natural as if it were the spiritual. Old Testament examples of this practice include the sacrifice of lambs and the observation of the dietary laws.

In the New Testament, examples include the Lord's Supper, water baptism, and the tithe, which have been taught only as archetypal practices without spiritual revelation. Religious practitioners cleave to these practices as if the truth of them is contained within the practice itself with no truth beyond the acts. Without the understanding of revelation as to the realties, truths, or mysteries veiled by the mere practices, they are perpetually infants, unequipped to adequately represent God to the world. The religious spirit's response, then, to the spirit of man's inquires into deep things of God, is to claim either that the religious practice itself holds value because it is the thing that God loves and rewards, or that such deeper understanding is unknowable.

Within this context, the sacrifice of the lamb became to those who only see through the eyes of the soul a central part of a national identity. The practice is linked to important historical commemorations, and has taken on the significance of a feast that unifies a people around a common heritage. Stripped of its divine relevance, the sacrifice of a lamb is reduced to an observance, hollowed out of its original meaning.

Well before nations existed, Abel sacrificed a lamb; and before Abraham's descendents became "as numerous as the stars of the heavens," a lamb was substituted for his son Isaac.[160] Forty-two generations later, the prophet John the Baptist would declare that Jesus was the "Lamb of God," come to be sacrificed for the sins of the world. Through the person of Jesus, God revealed the mystery surrounding the sacrifice of lambs, which had become inseparable from religious practice throughout the history of human civilization.

Apart from this truth, the killing of lambs for religious purposes has no intrinsic value. However, where a culture is held together through a ritual observation, the desire to perpetuate that culture overrides the willingness to abandon the practice, even in favor of the superseding glory of the reality that has fully appeared. By cultural and religious traditions, the practice becomes more valuable than the reality.

God intended that the copy or shadow of the heavenly reality remain in place only until the time for the reality arrives and the reality reveals God's true intentions. In the example of the priests who served in the tabernacle, and subsequently in the temple in Jerusalem, it is said that "they serve[d] at a sanctuary that is a copy and shadow of what is in heaven,"[161] and that "the Holy Spirit was showing by this that the way into the Most Holy Place had not yet been disclosed as long as the first tabernacle was still standing."[162] God does not empower both the shadow and the reality at the same time. Such a duality is both unnecessary and would cause confusion, and "...God is not the author of confusion, but of peace."[163]

THE VALUE OF REALITY

The value of the reality cannot be compared to that of the shadow. However, the shadows permit human interpretation, whereas the Spirit is the arbiter of the true reality. Those who are established in religious traditions as the pontifex[164] between heaven and earth have no interest in the advent of the reality. The coming of the reality transcends the limitations of the archetypes of religious and cultural traditions, and uniformly upsets the systems of authority by which their interpretation and practice are determined. Revelation always renders an institution built upon the foundation of the shadow irrelevant and threatens any such institution with extinction.

God knew that, after the fall, man would begin to see all things through his soul, which would hang over his understanding as a veil. Yet God's purposes for humankind that He had ordained from the beginning would continue until all such purposes had been fully accomplished. It would simply be a matter of time before the full intent of God would appear upon the earth, the realms of heaven and of earth would be united under the rule of one king, and the Kingdom of Heaven would appear upon the earth in the same fashion in which it existed in heaven. "[H]e made known to us the mystery of his will according to his good pleasure, which he purposed in Christ, to be put into effect when the times reach their fulfillment—to bring unity to all things in heaven and on earth under Christ."[165]

The Kingdom is not manifested in physical symbols, such as food and drink, but in a form of rule that is righteous and results in peace among those within its domain, "For the kingdom of God is not a matter of eating and drinking, but of righteousness, peace and joy in the Holy Spirit."[166] God continued to prepare men for the revelation of His Kingdom by inserting these divine reminders into the center of human culture. These divine symbols would remain in human culture, long after the knowledge of their significance had been lost to the human race.

However, the mere existence of the symbols predisposes humankind to receive God's true meaning, His intended purposes, when it is time for the realities underlying the symbols to appear on the earth. As the time for the appearing of the spiritual reality draws near, there also arises a corresponding longing for these truths to appear, whether or not humankind can actually identify or understand the thing for which they are longing.

If there is a natural body, there is also a spiritual body. So it is written: "The first man Adam became a living being"; the last Adam, a life-giving spirit. The spiritual did not come first, but the natural, and after that the spiritual. The first man was of the dust of the earth; the second man is of heaven. As was the earthly man, so are those who are of the earth; and as is the heavenly man, so also are those who are of heaven. And just as we have borne the image of the earthly man, so shall we bear the image of the heavenly man.[167]

THE PROMISE OF A KING

The loss of the first Adam's dominion could only be repaired by the restoration of rule through the last Adam. The loss of dominion meant that his purpose in creation changed from that of a ruler to a survivor. God's plan from the beginning was to send a second King to restore the culture of rule to His House. From the beginning of prophetic Scripture, the restoration of the relationship between God and man was meant to be accomplished through Jesus Christ, the King.

Satan was aware that God's plan was "to destroy the devil's work."[168] Christ would destroy man's dependence upon the systems of the *kosmos* through the reintroduction of a different Kingdom. As King, he would have the authority to cancel the consequences of men's sins and to rescue them from the domain of Satan and receive them into His own Kingdom.

All kingdoms are based upon some form of authority. The term "kingdom" means a foundation or basis of power and rule.[169] As such, a kingdom exists because a particular sovereign possesses the requisite authority to guarantee the safety and well-being of his subjects against all opposing forces. That authority not only provides provision and protection for the subjects of the king, but more importantly, it exists to support the subjects in a more primary undertaking.

In anticipation of Jesus' coming as King, prophetic Scripture lays out a clear path that keeps this preeminent focus throughout the Bible. Types and shadows representing this truth are not limited to objects in creation, but are the underlying message in numerous stories in the Old Testament. Two examples of which are Jacob's blessing of Judah and the specific inclusion of the woman Tamar in the genealogy of Christ. When Jacob comes to the end of his life and is blessing his sons, his prophecy over Judah is to acknowledge his line as the lineage of the King. He says:

> *Judah, your brothers will praise you; your hand will be on the neck of your enemies; your father's sons will bow down to you. You are a lion's cub, Judah; you return from the prey, my son. Like a lion he crouches and lies down, like a lioness—who dares to rouse him? The scepter will not depart from Judah, nor the ruler's staff from between his feet, until he to whom it belongs shall come and the obedience of the nations shall be his. He will tether his donkey to a vine, his colt to the choicest branch; he will wash his garments in wine, his robes in the blood of grapes. His eyes will be darker than wine, his teeth whiter than milk.*[170]

Jacob is identifying Judah as the one among his twelve sons who is chosen, through whose family line the promised King would come.

Judah was neither Jacob's favorite child nor his firstborn. By those criteria, Jacob would have chosen Joseph, his favorite, or Ruben, his firstborn, whom he knowingly bypassed, saying, "Ruben, you are my firstborn, my might, the first sign of my strength...."[171] Jacob did not choose Judah; he was chosen by God.

Judah was the one through whom the King would come, because he demonstrated the characteristics consistent with the purpose for the existence of Abraham's family. This is demonstrated in Ruben's and Judah's respective oaths to return Benjamin and Simeon from Egypt. To convince Jacob to send Benjamin to Egypt, so they could buy grain and free their brother Simeon, Ruben and Judah alternatively made pledges for Benjamin's safety. Ruben offered the lives of both of his sons as surety against Benjamin's safety, but Jacob rejected this oath.[172] Judah, however, guaranteed the sons' safe return with his own life.[173] In this pledge, Judah prefigures the requirements necessary for the redeeming of all the sons of God back to the Father, which requirements Jesus would actually fulfill.

Unlike Ruben, Judah embodied the essential characteristics of Christ by pledging his life as a guarantee that he would return the captive sons of Jacob. Ruben not only preferred his own life to the lives of his children, but he was also willing to put his lineage at risk. He could not, therefore, be trusted to preserve the line of the King. On the other hand, Judah's pledge was more consistent with the spirit of self-sacrifice that would be fully embodied in Christ. He, therefore, is more emblematic of the culture of the house of Abraham than his older brother Ruben.

Similarly, the story of Tamar shows a dedication to the preservation of the line of the King. Judah was reluctant to honor Tamar's right to raise a son to carry on the promise of Abraham's family, but God honored Tamar's persistence. Her resolute behavior broke through all barriers and allowed her the right to be tied to this family and to its divine purpose. In her story, she required two pledges from Judah: his staff and his signet ring, the twin symbols of his authority. The staff of Judah represented the scepter in the hand of the King that would come from his bloodline. The signet ring was the symbol of his authority. She valued the things that God valued and was therefore accorded the right to keep the line of Judah alive. In honor of her persistence in preserving the life of the king, she is permanently installed in the record of the genealogy of Christ. God gave her twin sons and named one Perez,[174] which means the one who breaks through.[175] He is the offspring through whom Jesus comes.

These stories are types and shadows given to provide insight into the mind of the Lord and as illustrations that the ways of God are both knowable and reliable.

On Earth as it Is in Heaven

As has been noted earlier, every aspect of the order of creation, whether grand or seemingly insignificant, is connected to a heavenly antecedent. Similarly, every story in the Scriptures is strategically placed to illuminate a path that reliably progresses to disclose an end known from the beginning. Types and shadows, therefore, are found in both the natural world and in the chronicle of Scripture. They represent the consistent unfolding of the mysteries of heaven.

God structured it this way because he knew that man would sin, and in that condition man could only see and understand heavenly things in a veiled way. He would be distracted by his obsessive search for provision and protection and would stumble over profound truths about the purposes of God without recognizing their value. Yet, God would continue to speak to him and would maintain a connection between man's culture and eternal realities through these types and shadows.

When the King came, however, He was the light of the world, because the meaning of all the forms of types and shadows are illuminated through His word and His person. He is the new template for the deconstruction of all the mysteries hidden in the types and shadows. Upon His return to heaven, He sent the Spirit of Truth, which was in Him while He was in the earth, to coexist with the spirit within man. The same Spirit animated the spirit of man and brought about the same revelation that Jesus came to present.

By the Spirit, the mysteries hidden in types and shadows are disclosed so that one who is led by the spirit may clearly understand what Jesus meant to convey. The types and shadows in both the natural world and the statements of Scripture act as reliable confirmation of the accuracy of a believer's understanding of the person of Christ. "For everything that was written in the past was written to teach us, so that through the endurance taught in the Scriptures and the encouragement they provide, we might have hope."[176]

God always intended that man should know Him. Despite his

devolution into sin, God retained a strong connection to the being of man, speaking to him as completely as his soul could understand. Since God always planned to restore a primary connection to the spirit of man, the things spoken to his soul were calculated to keep him aware of basic things about God until the day when he could replace his soul under the rule of his spirit, and the eyes of his spirit would be reopened.

The battle for the reality of man's vision of God was lost in the Garden of Eden, but was regained in the garden of Gethsemane. In the Garden of Eden, the eyes of the soul were opened and from then on a veil was erected between God and the first Adam. However, in the garden of Gethsemane, the last Adam declared that His spirit was willing to trust God through the looming events of the cross.

My Father! My Father!

CHAPTER 10

Father and Sons

...Adam, the son of God.[177]

"Son" is the term that describes an issue out of the person of a father. To impart one's image and likeness to another is simultaneously the greatest act of generosity and the most complete expression of goodness. To be inextricably bound to another whose being defines, at least in part, the future of the relationship is an act of supreme humility, especially when the Father is God and the son is man.

The most profound aspect of the character of God is that of Father. God as Father expresses completely His nature of love: the love of God is inseparable from its expression as Father, and the nature of Father is inseparable from the character of love, particularly when fathering is by design.

God conceived of man as His son deliberately to express the nature of love. His careful attentiveness of this purpose explains why God would enter into a covenant with Himself to benefit man before He created Him. Man was not designed as merely a continually evolving protoplasmic flotsam, adrift in the vastness of the universe. God tied His own being to man by His unbreakable oath to Himself. In the creation of man, He set forth a proving ground for the demonstration of His nature of love. Although God always had in mind to put the majesty of His love on display, the depths of His love could not fully be displayed until He created a Son in His own image and likeness.

This process exists due to the nature of love. Love does not exist merely as a theory or concept. For love to exist, it must be actualized—expressed and tested. Love may be demonstrated in a variety of ways. In the Kingdom of God, such demonstrations exist as forms of order and governance that benefit all who are within the Kingdom. However, love is presented perfectly within the context of a father and his children, because that is the only form in which the nature of love, as defined by God's relationship to man, can be fully tested and, therefore, fully expressed.

God's relationship to man, as Father to sons, is neither accidental nor casual. It is a deliberate order and foreordained by God. God decided to create man as His son; man was powerless to influence this decision in any way.

The love of God for man is the foundation for man's purpose in creation. When man separated himself from his Father, his purpose in creation was lost. It is only by being reconciled to his Father that he may regain the true purpose for being. The love of God should never be construed as the basis for permitting man to engage in reckless and dissolute behavior without consequence. For indeed, such a fashion of life has consequences, both in time and the hereafter. These profound truths about the nature of God and His purpose for creating man seem contrary to the normal religious emphasis of the unworthiness of man, as the background against which to view the charity of God.

Prior to the coming of Christ and man's restoration to sonship, man's purpose in creation was defined by this hope of redemption. Accordingly, in this time of types and shadows, God favored certain behaviors, the significance of which were largely unrecognized by the participants. People were allowed to engage in religious activities that mimicked principles of father and son relationships, preserving the purpose for creation and the hope of redemption in the culture.

For example, Abraham did not understand why God would ask him to go through the preparations of sacrificing Isaac, then stay his hand at the last moment and provide a sacrifice Himself. However, his willingness to proceed as far as he did showed the heart of God the Father, who was willing to sacrifice Jesus to save Adam. On the basis of that undertaking, then, God qualified Abraham to be the recipient of the promise to bring Christ into the world through his lineage.[178]

One should not construe this hope of restoration nor the restoration to sonship through Christ as the end within itself. The restoration of man through Christ is primarily a restoration to his lost state. It is a repositioning of man. God made man as a son, and Christ restored him to sonship. The restoration to sonship is God's provision for accurately realigning man in the earth so that God may put on display the true meaning of Father through him.

Just as a son needs a father in order to properly understand his identity and his purpose, a father requires a son in order to put on display the father's nature. A son's history and his origin are determined by the father out of whom the son issued. Accordingly, his purpose can never be furthered in contradistinction from his father. Correspondingly, the father is pledged to support the existence of his son. This is the role God chose when He created the son to put His nature on display. Father and son, therefore, is a symbiotic and intricately interconnected relationship toward a mutual and continuing purpose.

Before the coming of Christ, however, the fatherless culture had permeated every aspect of human interaction, and it was rare to find a true picture of God the Father in human traditions. That this foundational aspect of heavenly culture was singularly absent on earth necessitated the advent of a model to guide man in his understanding back to the standard of father and son. God sent Jesus, His Son, to live among humans for precisely this purpose— to provide a template against which this restored relationship could be understood and measured. The imagination of man could not replicate this essential culture. It had to become visible again through Jesus' pristine heavenly model.

BORN AGAIN

The salvation of man comprises the tasks of rescuing him from the culture of the orphan and restoring him to the culture of a son of God. The process involves rescuing him from his reliance upon his soul, which reliance entraps him in Satan's kingdom.

The Kingdom of God is a safe haven of authority, rooted in the sovereignty of Christ. It is an environment in which one's spirit regains control over his soul. The process of being translated into the Kingdom of God is described as being "born again of the spirit."

As with any birth, the original coming forth is in an infantile state. The newborn son goes through distinct stages of growth and maturity before he becomes capable of functioning in the culture of heaven. In this transition, he is aided primarily by the Holy Spirit, who retrofits his spirit with characteristics that are distinctly heavenly in origin.

There are seven distinct characteristics of the Holy Spirit that Jesus displayed as the model to inform the progression of an infant son to maturity. The seven characteristics of the Spirit result in the restoration of rule. They are the Spirit of the Lord, wisdom, understanding, counsel, power, knowledge, and the reverential regard for the nature of God.[179] Although these characteristics may have their earthly counterparts, their source is divine and they function to change man's fundamental nature from carnal to divine. Through the stages of growth as a son, these seven characteristics begin to be more pronounced, commensurate with the maturing of the son.

A mature son is produced by a deliberate process. One is born again of spirit in order to restore the original balance of the spirit's dominance over the soul. Being born again of the Spirit is not by itself the indication of maturity, but the restoration of this condition is required in order for maturity to occur.

The process for the maturing of sons of God is stewarded within the order and arrangement of the House of God. Unlike an orphan, a son represents continuity in his generation and carries forward the purposes for which a family exists. The House of God derives its relevance from God Himself. In every successive generation, God reveals Himself more completely until He is fully disclosed. Whereas the purpose of an orphan is always completed within the span of his own lifetime, a son's destiny represents the ongoing disclosure of the purpose of the house to which he belongs. Therefore, the purpose of a son, though unique in its expression, is intimately tied to a predetermined purpose. "The son is the radiance of God's glory and the exact representation of his being."[180] Every son was designed to present a unique feature of his father's nature, and all the sons together make up the complete expression of the Father's family in the earth in any epoch of time.

This is the critical framework by which a son is restored to mature functionality, and is suitably positioned to engage God's original intent for him. Each son is raised to maturity to present a unique picture of a particular facet of the Father. The purpose of each son is to radiate his Father's glory and to represent Him exactly. Corporately, through the House of God, multiple facets of God's nature are revealed until, ultimately, God reveals Himself completely in the closing age of man.

THE RADIANCE OF HIS FATHER'S GLORY

God intends to convey His love to humankind in every generation. Certain aspects of His love, such as Jesus' death on the cross, have been permanently presented. Jesus' death displayed the love of God in all of its fullness, once for all time, and the availability of this truth to all the generations since that defining event has continued. The nature of God displayed in that moment was meant to resonate within human beings wherever and whenever they live. God deploys His children to every facet of human existence, so that through them the face of His love might be presented throughout the earth in every generation.

The love of God is not only a story from antiquity, but exists currently in the lives of the sons of God. "For you died and your life is now hidden with God in Christ. When Christ, who is your life, appears, then you will also appear with him in glory."[181] The sons, in turn, are deployed to give both form and substance to the reality of God and to the truth of the message of the cross. By displaying acts of His goodness, the sons demonstrate the love of God among humankind on an everyday basis. The relationship between the Father and the Son provides for the appropriate format from which God's glory may radiate in the earth.

God's glory is His goodness. It is not the dazzling light that surrounds Him, nor is it His awesome power to create. The dazzling light that surrounds Him is His ordinary environment, and His competence to speak the universe into being is not extraordinary for His creative abilities. As stupendous as these qualities are to us, they are not noteworthy to God. God is singularly unimpressed when we reference the brightness of His environment and enumerate long lists of His accomplishments.

If we were to worship God because He wraps Himself in light, or because of His unimaginable power to create, our worship would be rooted in dread and fear of Him. There would be nothing that would distinguish the worship of God as Father from that form of worship offered to false gods, motivated by a desire to avoid their wrath and secure their favor through offerings and sacrifices. He would be no different from the impersonal gods of pagan mythology to whom their devotees gave obeisance based upon the putative threats to one's welfare and the ire of powerful beings. God does not need the assurance of humans that His creative accomplishments entitle Him to their worship. Everything He made was done before He created man. So, the creation testifies to man about the existence of God and the beauty of His order.

It is God's goodness that best describes His glory. When Moses requested of the Lord, "Now show me your glory,"[182] God replied:

> *I will cause all my goodness to pass in front of you, and I will*
> *proclaim my name, the LORD, in your presence. I will have*
> *mercy on whom I will have mercy, and I will have compassion*
> *on whom I will have compassion. ...There is a place near me*
> *where you may stand on a rock. When my glory passes by, I*
> *will put you in a cleft in the rock and cover you with my hand*
> *until I have passed by.*[183]

When the event occurred, the Lord came down in a cloud and stood before Moses.

> *Then the LORD came down in the cloud and stood there with*
> *him and proclaimed his name, the LORD. And he passed*
> *in front of Moses, proclaiming, "The LORD, the LORD, the*
> *compassionate and gracious God, slow to anger, abounding in*
> *love and faithfulness, maintaining love to thousands, and for-*
> *giving wickedness, rebellion and sin. Yet he does not leave the*
> *guilty unpunished; he punishes the children and their children*
> *for the sin of the fathers to the third and fourth generation."*
> *Moses bowed to the ground at once and worshiped.*[184]

The event acts like a formal introduction in which God presents Himself to Moses, because Moses had found favor with the Lord. God described Himself in the encounter by emphasizing His com-passion, grace, patience, steadfast love and faithfulness, and His forgiveness, while maintaining righteousness despite generations of resistance to His plan and will. God showed Himself not by His fierce countenance nor by His awesome majesty, but by the declaration of His goodness. God chose to be known for His all-surpassing goodness.

God has never chosen to distance Himself from man. Instead, He has consistently chosen a relationship of intimacy with man. As a Father with His own offspring, He has sought to infuse His nature into the very being of man—from the beginning when He squeezed the form of man out of the dust of the ground, He breathed spirit out of His own person into the container of clay.

Throughout His dealings with humankind, God's standard pattern has been His search for an intimate connection to man. Whether His unsuccessful approach of Israel on Mount Sinai,[185] or His perfect contact through Jesus,[186] His desire to present His goodness has been constant in His outreach to man.

By contrast, religious cultures tend to operate based on the presumption that the respective deity is distant from man and is unknowable. Some representations, even within the Christian faith, continue to view God through this common religious mindset, considering familiarity with God disrespectful, and borderline blasphemous. This point of view, however, is inconsistent with God's historic approach to man, as well as His present intent.

When the original son required rescuing, God Himself came, clothed in human flesh, to restore the original position of sonship. The form of a son is necessary to accommodate the purpose for which God created man: to show the nature of the Father. God in Jesus shows the intimate, knowable nature of God; that is why Jesus could say, "The works that I do are not my own, it is the Father living in me who is doing his work."[187] So, Jesus, in His earthly life, became the pattern for all sons, "[And] we beheld his glory, the glory as of the only begotten of the Father, full of grace and truth."[188]

A LIVING SACRIFICE

The ultimate demonstration of the goodness of God displayed through the person of Jesus, the Son, was on the cross. Jesus' viewpoint on the impending event was clear. He said, "Father… glorify your Son, that your Son may glorify you."[189] In that instant, the presentation of the glory of God through the person of Jesus Christ consumed the life of Jesus Himself, but simultaneously put on display the ultimate standard of love. God chose to love the son who strayed away from Him enough to consume the life of the Son who remained obedient to Him in order to rescue the errant son, who at the time that God made this decision hated God. God's love is circumscribed in this event, and it reveals the depths of His goodness. His choice was entirely benevolent in that He sacrificed the Son who loved Him to save the one who despised Him, uninfluenced by any benefit to Him. This is pure goodness.

When someone loves another enough to sacrifice his life for the other, while the other hates him, there is a total absence of selfish motivation for this behavior. In that scenario, the purity of one's love is undeniable. The display of such goodness shows the glory of one's nature.

To that end, all believers are called to the standard of sonship established by Jesus Christ. He was completely available to the Father as a source from which the glory of the Father could radiate in the earth. Following His example, the Scriptures urge believers, "offer your bodies as a living sacrifice, holy and pleasing to God—this is your true and proper worship."[190]

As a living sacrifice, every believer is called to a life in which the priority is to put on display the goodness of God within the measures of one's rule. When God put Adam in creation with the mandate to rule, His intent was that the earth should benefit from the way that a son of God presented the goodness of God in his rule. For example, in Jesus' representation of the Father's character, "we beheld His glory…as the only begotten of the Father, full of grace and truth."[191] When He raised Lazarus from the dead, He explained His actions to Martha, "Did I not tell you that if you believed, you would see the glory of God?"[192] Even His death on the cross is explained as the act by which He most clearly puts on display the glory of the Father. The world was given the opportunity to observe the goodness of God through Jesus' rule.

ADMINISTRATIONS

Administrations are designed to give force and effect to a preexisting philosophy of rule, and the philosophy of the rule underlies the structure of the administration of power. The condition of the subjects of a ruler is the best indication of the character of the sovereign, and the administration of his rule. When God set Adam over creation, his intent was that Adam would reflect the culture of the house to which he belonged as a son. It was God's design that He would put on display His own goodness though the agency of His son in the form of the governmental order He introduced to the earth. That order was not designed to function through legislative decrees and bureaucracies, but through the administration of the simple and elegant flow of fathers and sons.

The entire human race was organized under Adam's administration through patriarchal relationships for the first millennium of man's existence on earth. Although Adam sinned, God still kept him at the helm of human society for almost one thousand years. One thousand years was long enough for this model to take root among the tribal societies as they were being formed into what would, ultimately, become nations. Even in his rebellion against his Father, Adam was still useful to establish a form of order that was a type and shadow of the heavenly government.

Christ fully established the model of God's intent to present His goodness to humankind through His sons and has passed that legacy on to the succeeding generations of the sons of God upon the earth. Whereas, no individual son is assigned the vastness of the scope previously conveyed to both Christ and Adam, it is nevertheless unmistakable that all sons have been given a sphere of rule in which they are commissioned and empowered to put on display the glory of their Father's love.

The vastness of the role of displaying God's goodness, committed to the hands of Jesus, is carried on in the earth in the corporate Body of Christ. Jesus described that work as being even greater in scope than what He individually undertook. In its completeness, the representation of the goodness of God by the corporate Christ will be inclusive of the portions given to both the first and last Adam, but empowered by the Holy Spirit. The glory of that expression will be a complete model on the earth of what exists in heaven.

THE EXACT REPRESENTATION OF HIS BEING

God brings a son to maturity not only to express His goodness through the son, but also to empower the son to act on behalf of the Father in such a way that "the Father judges no one, but has entrusted all judgment to the Son, that all may honor the Son just as they honor the Father…."[193] A mature son, therefore, is meant to speak and to act on behalf of the Father as His designated agent.

The mature son is capable of accurately and consistently discerning the Father's intent, and of executing that intent precisely. "Do not conform to the pattern of this world, but be transformed by the renewing of your mind. Then you will be able to test and approve what God's will is—his good, pleasing and perfect will."[194] The process by which the mature son is able to distinguish between the levels of God's will, ranging from the good to the perfect, is by the renewing of the mind. The Holy Spirit works to restore the soul of man to its proper place of submission to his spirit. The renewing of the mind that follows is the reassertion of the mind of his spirit over the mind of his soul, permitting the flow of information from the Holy Spirit to the mind of the man's spirit. The effect is to transform his view of reality. The result is a perfect realignment between the mind of man and the will of God.

Concurrent with this repositioning, the mature son is also empowered by the wisdom of the Holy Spirit to know how to precisely execute the Father's commands, "[f]or the Father loves the Son and shows him all he does."[195]

Presently, the difficulty in envisioning this form of interaction between God and man is caused by the continuing influence of the culture of the orphan, which perceives a wide chasm of separation between God and man, even in those who are said to be born again. The culture of the orphan is inherently competitive and emphasizes the difference between God and man.

The culture of the son embraces the truth of the reconciliation of the Father and the son and the re-issuance of the nature of spirit in the son that makes him compatible with the Holy Spirit. He is defined by sameness of being with the Father and no longer by any form of competitive distinctiveness. Jesus, being the model of sonship, showed that between man and His Father, there is no competition:

> *In your relationships with one another, have the same attitude of mind Christ Jesus had:*
> *Who, being in very nature God, did not consider equality with God something to be used to his own advantage; rather, he made himself nothing by taking the very nature of a servant, being made in human likeness. And being found in appearance as a human being, he humbled himself by becoming obedient to death—even death on a cross! Therefore God exalted him to the highest place and gave him the name that is above every name, that at the name of Jesus every knee should bow, in heaven and on earth and under the earth, and every tongue acknowledge that Jesus Christ is Lord, to the glory of God the Father.*[196]

When Jesus was on the earth, he did not assert equality with God as the basis for His life or actions, although He could have since He was God in human form. Instead, He is the model that illustrates to man how a son may be the exact representation of his Father's being. Had He asserted His equality with God, all of what He did would have demonstrated His own competence; His model would be unattainable by man, and He could only have been viewed as His gift of labor to the Father. He would have indebted God to Himself, and all benefit to us would have shown only the kindness of Jesus to us. The nature of the Father would have remained a mystery. Instead, by choosing to do nothing except represent the goodness of the Father, He put on display the nature of the Father.

The highest attainment possible within a competitive standard is equality, and fairness is the principle objective in a system of competition. In such a system, righteousness is understood only in terms of fairness. There is no basis in relationships for trans-generational building within an environment of competition. The relationship between a father and a son cannot be expressed within the context of competition. The goal of everyone within this system is to acquire his independent estate.

According to this mindset, all exchanges between God and man assume equality between the parties. Man offers his service to God on the presumption that such services are required and necessary and that God will accept the service as an offering. This view, of necessity, obligates God to a response. Any failure on God's part to respond would leave Him indebted to man since He has received a benefit for which He has not adequately compensated man. Whether God responds by giving man an adequate compensation or simply remains indebted, the work of man elevates him to a position of equality with God, since God accepted his work. Therefore, man may offer his resources to God as the offering of his righteousness.

A RIGHTEOUS OFFERING

This form of bargain holds that the righteousness of man may be offered in an exchange with God. On the basis of this concept, God's rejection of the sacrifice of Cain does not appear to have any explanation except to suggest that perhaps God is at times whimsical, arbitrary, or even capricious; a view that is entirely inconsistent with the Scriptures.

The least attractive aspect of this system, however, is that any suggestion of a relationship based upon the mutuality of exchange does not permit the Father to function through the son and does not give the son access to the resources of the Father on the basis of being His heir. This is not the model that Jesus established. Jesus described His relationship with the Father as "you are in me and I am in you,"[197] signifying that the Father worked from His location within the being of the Son, and the Son operated from deep within the authority of His Father.

Exact representation, therefore, like radiating the glory of the Father's nature, is the designated goal of sonship. One is not born again only to be restored to the position of son, but also to the practical functioning of that role.

The standard for mature sonship, established by Jesus, is seen when the son permits his life to be consumed by the Father in order to set forth the perfect standard of the Father's love and declares the will of the Father exactly as the Father Himself would. In the earth, the will of the Father is pursued through the mature son. "[The Son] is the image of the invisible God, the firstborn over all creation. …For God was pleased to have all his fullness dwell in him, and through him to reconcile to himself all things, whether things on earth or things in heaven, by making peace through his blood, shed on the cross."[198] The work of representing the Father in the earth has been committed into the hands of the son, and the Holy Spirit was given to reveal the will of the Father and to empower the son.

> *[T]hat God was reconciling the world to himself in Christ, not counting people's sins against them. And he has committed to us the message of reconciliation. We are therefore Christ's ambassadors, as though God were making his appeal through us. We implore you on Christ's behalf: Be reconciled to God. God made him who had no sin to be sin for us, so that in him we might become the righteousness of God.*[199]

CHAPTER 11

Functioning as Fathers and Sons

Jesus fully presented an understanding of a true relationship with God as Father. Adam's early departure from this intended relationship to God left unshown God's intended relationship to man as sons. Adam's default to the culture of the fatherless provided no foundation for humankind to live in relationship to God as a Father whom he loves and trusts.

The Gospels, however, introduce Jesus Christ as the Son of God and presented to humankind with the declared purpose of finishing all that was lacking with his predecessor, Adam. The records of Luke and Matthew introduce Jesus through complete and deliberate genealogical records. Luke presents Jesus as the Son of God, descended from Adam through an unbroken line of sixty-two generations. Matthew's record shows Him as both the King, descended from David of the house of Judah, and the fulfillment of the promise to Abraham, as the seed through whom the precreation covenant would be fulfilled upon the earth.

The introduction to the Gospel of John identifies Jesus as the preexistent Word of God by whom the universe was formed and who appears as the incarnate God "full of grace and truth."[200] The fourth writer of the Gospel is Mark, the scribe recording the message of Jesus from the apostle Peter, and his message is unmistakable. He writes, "The beginning of the gospel about Jesus Christ, the

Son of God," and opens with the story of God authenticating Jesus as His Son on the occasion of His baptism by John in the river Jordan. "As Jesus was coming up out of the water, he saw heaven being torn open and the Spirit descending on him like a dove. And a voice came from heaven: 'You are my Son, whom I love; with you I am well pleased.'"[201]

The purpose of Jesus' coming into the earth included fulfilling the requirements of the precreation covenant, but His life was also meant to fully demonstrate how the Son of God, born into the world of human beings as an infant, would progress through the stages of a human life. Though ultimately He was killed on the cross, was resurrected from the dead, and ascended to heaven, Jesus' life provides a history filled with details about the Son of God and His relationship to His Father. This life was designed to be a template for understanding how God relates to His sons and how sons of God are meant to relate to the everlasting Father. Jesus' life filled the void that Adam left regarding a model for understanding the relationship between man as a son of God and God the Father.

When Adam defaulted to the position of being alone in the world, without a Father, God acknowledged that Adam's condition entitled him to the bread of his own toil.[202] Adam's separation from his Father also resulted in a separation from the estate designed to supply him in this way. He and his progeny came to rely instead upon the force of their own strength and their skill in the development and use of technology.

As a son of God, Adam had been entitled to the support of his Father's house while he attended the rule to which he was assigned, and the Kingdom that he represented was sufficient to supply all of his needs for resourcing so that his rule would not be deficient in any manner. His Father would supply his need for wisdom, knowledge, council, understanding, and power, all key elements necessary for his successful administration.

God would have conveyed this supply both directly and indirectly. Direct conveyance would have occurred by Spirit to spirit contact. Indirectly, supply was already present in the order and structure of creation around him, which Adam would have called forth. The relationship of sonship, in which the Father loves the son and the son trusts the Father, is required for this order of rule and supply to function.

The relationship between Jesus and God the Father shows this relationship perfectly. Although the Father remains invisible, His divine goodness is resplendently displayed through the words and works of Jesus. For His part, Jesus clothed Himself in the role of a son, affording humanity a complete picture of the order of the relationship that God envisioned when He made man as His son. Therefore, Jesus' life is the intended point of reference for understanding the father and son relationship as God originally intended it.

A CHILD IS BORN

Extreme hostility opposed Jesus' introduction into the world. Satan arranged to have Him killed upon arrival via King Herod, the ruler of Israel at the time of Jesus' birth, who had shown previously that he would suffer no potential challenges to his rule. Herod was known for his murderous elimination of any opposition to his rule.[203] God did not employ divine prerogatives to influence favorably the circumstances of Jesus' arrival, since those benefits would be typically unavailable to the normal human birth.

Rather, the Father introduced the Son in the most austere circumstances. Although some choose to see the circumstances of Jesus' birth as a glorification of poverty, it is properly understood as an evasive strategy that allowed the Son to arrive, undetected by the enemy, while meeting the test of circumstances into which humans might be born. The Father took advantage of Satan's pride and his inability to envision the Son of God arriving in such humble and meager circumstances. The enemy was not looking for the King of kings in a stable, born among the animals.

Similarly, when Herod continues his unrelenting persecution of Christ by killing the children, God instructed Joseph to hide the family in Egypt until Herod's death. For a Jewish person, residence in Egypt was reminiscent of their tenure as slaves in that country. Satan, being oblivious to the prophetic significance of the nation of Israel as a type and shadow of Jesus, being formerly enslaved in and delivered from Egypt, could not see the significance of Jesus following the same path in order to fulfill the prophecy, "Out of Egypt I called my son."[204] God simultaneously protected the Son and fulfilled prophecy, thereby authenticating Jesus as the actual fulfillment of the prophetic word.

The circumstances of Jesus' birth demonstrate the role of the Father in presenting a son. The Father protected the Son even as He developed the unimpeachable testimony that supported Jesus' claim to be the Son of God. He did this through evidence that Jesus Himself could neither perpetrate nor influence.

The early events of Jesus' life show this same quality of relationship between Himself and the Father. As soon as Jesus had the capacity to respond to God as a son, He began to seek understanding of His Father. It was the custom for a boy, at the age of twelve, to take up an apprenticeship in his father's business. When at twelve, Jesus accompanied His parents to Jerusalem. He remained behind in the temple to consult with the learned scholars, telling Mary He did so because he "must be about [his] Father's business."[205] Jesus knew that although Joseph fulfilled the role of an earthly father, God was His true Father and, at His age, His responsibility was to take up an apprenticeship in His Father's business. The doctors of the law in the temple were the best and most complete source of information available to help Him understand the nature of His Father's business. He had enough clarity of understanding to seek the most complete understanding of His identity and purpose from the custodians of that knowledge.

Jesus' life from the age of twelve until He was thirty years old is summarized in the statement, "Jesus grew in wisdom and stature, and in favor with God and men."[206] Paul would also write about Jesus, "Although he was a son, he learned obedience from what he suffered.[207] The Father permitted every form of trial to which a human being would be subjected to attend Jesus, while God carefully monitored His progress and gave Him what help He needed. The Father did not simply abandon Jesus to the circumstances of life until He was thirty. Jesus' path was laid out carefully so that His sufferings and trials would install the layers of obedience necessary to sustain the pressure of His destiny.[208] God's intent was to prepare Him for the time of His maturity through the incidences that shaped the quality of His responses. The things He suffered were related directly to the specific obedience to the Father required by His unique destiny. The Father's involvement in the process is clear and unambiguous. Jesus grew in favor with God as He submitted Himself to the leading of the Spirit and to the instruction of Scripture, both of which informed His choices consistently.

God put the results of Jesus' training on display for us to observe when, immediately after His baptism, the Holy Spirit led Jesus into the wilderness to be tempted by the devil.[209] In the three recorded temptations, Jesus responded to the enemy on the strength of the word of the Spirit applicable to the circumstance. He verified that word by the use of scriptural text. However, when Satan attempted to subvert this process by himself employing the Scriptures, Jesus quickly distinguished this cunning use of Scripture meant to produce disobedience and death. Jesus restored the appropriate authority of Scripture, being familiar with the voice of the Spirit. Throughout His ministry, He would constantly show His familiarity with the Spirit in His use of Scripture and would distinguish the misuse of Scripture by those well-versed in the knowledge of the text, and the traditional interpretations, but oblivious to the Spirit.

The temptations and Jesus' responses reveal the results of the Father's deliberate preparation of the Son with full knowledge of the Son's destiny. Jesus' trials produced a dependence upon the Spirit of God, while employing the knowledge of the text of Scripture. This was His consistent pattern of response. His Father arranged the trials to take Him to increasingly higher levels of maturity and preparedness. These progressive increases were the evidence of His growing favor with God, and because He was clearly distinguished by His righteous responses, the favor of man also followed.

Moreover, God publicly declared to the world His pleasure in His Son's baptism by John when Jesus was thirty years old, declaring, "This is my Son, whom I love; with him I am well pleased."[210] This is not the declaration of an absent father who has reemerged after eighteen years, but the presentation of His Son as His designated heir and representative. Since God Himself had overseen every aspect of His training, He could testify to the world of Jesus' perfection. Christ was not sacrificed on the cross three and a half years later in order to be perfect in His obedience to the Father. Rather, it was His obedience for the preceding thirty years of His obscurity that made Him perfect and qualified Him to both represent the Father perfectly in His years of ministry and to be the unblemished Sacrifice on the cross.

Jesus' birth, early years, and presentation to the world demonstrate the hand of the Father in raising up a mature Son. Similarly, Jesus' three years of ministry provide a detailed look into the structure and function of the relationship between the Father and the Son.

Because Jesus came into the earth to fulfill a destiny that was determined for Him before the foundations of the world, the Father selected the time, place, and circumstances into which He would be placed. These were careful selections previously arranged to accommodate all the training and preparation necessary to make Him ready for His destiny. Jesus could choose how He responded to any of these preparations for His life, and if He were governed by His soul, He would naturally gravitate toward the circumstances that offered provision and protection. However, since He never departed from God, Jesus was always guided by the fellowship His Spirit had with the Holy Spirit who lived in him. Even from His childhood, He sought out the understanding of His destiny and pursued a pattern of choice and selection aimed at fulfilling His destiny. He, therefore, enjoyed the favor of both God and man.

The arrangement of Jesus' circumstances and His righteous choices within those circumstances are demonstrated in His ministry. The Father placed among the choices of Jesus' disciples Judas Iscariot, the one who would betray Him, and Jesus identified

Judas as a selection that God had given to Him: "I have revealed you to those whom you gave me out of the world. ...While I was with them, I protected them and kept them safe by that name you gave me. None has been lost except the one doomed to destruction so that Scripture would be fulfilled."[211] Jesus even gave God an account to include the outcome of Judas' betrayal. Yet, Jesus took responsibility for Judas as if He had selected him to be among the twelve. Jesus made this selection, knowing fully the nature of Judas. "Then Jesus replied, 'Have I not chosen you, the Twelve? Yet one of you is a devil!' (He meant Judas, the son of Simon Iscariot, who, though one of the Twelve, was later to betray him.)"[212]

In the model of the Father-Son relationship presented between God the Father and Jesus Christ the Son, the Father recognized that the Son had an eternal destiny for which He has come into the world. The Father's responsibility was to select and arrange the circumstances of the son's life to guide the fulfillment of this preexisting destiny. The Son's choices ranged from among the selections arranged by the Father, and did not include an infinite number of possible choices.

The Son's connection to the Father made Him aware of the need to make His selections according to the Spirit. Being led by the Spirit, the Son consistently chose in accordance with the perfect will of God. If, on the other hand, He had been governed by the will of His soul, His choices would have been informed primarily by the need to survive, and He would have been unaffected by the call to an eternal destiny. In that case, His choices would have been routinely different from those of His Father. He would remain untrained and, therefore, unqualified to fulfill an eternal destiny.

YOU ARE IN ME AND I AM IN YOU

My prayer is not for them alone. I pray also for those who will believe in me through their message, that all of them may be one, Father, just as you are in me and I am in you. May they also be in us so that the world may believe that you have sent me. I have given them the glory that you gave me, that they may be one as we are one—I in them and you in me—so that they may be brought to complete unity. Then the world will know that you sent me and have loved them even as you have loved me. Father, I want those you have given me to be with me where I am, and to see my glory, the glory you have given me because you loved me before the creation of the world. Righteous Father, though the world does not know you, I know you, and they know that you have sent me. I have made you known to them, and will continue to make you known in order that the love you have for me may be in them and that I myself may be in them.[213]

As His life on earth entered its final stage, just prior to the cross, Jesus described the relationship between Himself and the Father in this prayer to God. This description leaves no doubt that the life of Jesus was connected to the life within the Father in a virtually inseparable fashion. "You are in me" is an indication that Jesus presented Himself as a living sacrifice to host the presence of the Father. As Spirit, the Father could live in Jesus "both to will and to do of his good pleasure."[214] The Father prepared Jesus for the destiny of hosting the presence of God in an unobstructed way. No independent desire of Jesus' existed to compete with the use of His person by God. Jesus voluntarily submitted His whole being to God for whatever use God chose to make of it.

Jesus' choice on this part defines the trust a son has for his father. This trust is neither blind nor uninformed, since Jesus Himself was apprised fully of the eternal purpose that He was living out upon the earth. He trusted the love of His Father for Him and He firmly believed in the goodness of His Father toward mankind. He knew that He had come to be the Lamb, slain from the foundations of the world.

In order to trust God fully, every son needs to have a clear sense of what his divine destiny is designed to be. This prerequisite permits the son to agree with the Father's selections and to adopt them as his own willing and conscious choices. It was this process that allowed Jesus to conclude, "yet not my will, but yours be done."[215] The irony was that Jesus made a choice when He consented to the Father's will. That is why He could claim, then, "No one takes [my life] from me, but I lay it down of my own accord...."[216] It is also why the same choice that defines the love of God the Father also defines the manner in which Christ Himself loved: "Greater love has no one than this, that he lay down his life for his friends."[217] In the end, the work done by the Father through the Son is as readily attributable to the Son as it is to the Father. Therefore, it may be accurately said that "I and the Father are one."[218]

Before he has his own, separate independence, every son is in his father. God's intention is that the purpose of a son is to be the continuation of his father's identity. When Adam separated himself from his Father, this concept was lost to humanity, and independence replaced continuity in defining destiny. Even when it is clear that the destiny of each person is a unique expression of a preexisting, precreation plan, men are inclined to resist being defined by the life of anyone else. As a consequence, destiny is commonly considered apart from the unfolding of enormous purposes that require multigenerational participation in the same unfolding. Even large accomplishments within a single lifetime are quickly forgotten when those accomplishments are not part of an overarching purpose spanning many generations. Whereas, even a life that contributes modestly to the fulfillment of a grand purpose survives for a considerable period of time, because lives are meant to be associated with the fulfillment of eternal themes. In the case of God and Jesus, the great themes were established before the foundation of the world by the Father and the Son.

The particular arrangement of father and son was the necessary relational context to permit the engagement of this grand, eternal purpose in time. The Father determined how His love would be expressed within the venue He chose for that expression, and God took the roles of both Father and Son by which to express His divine nature. He planned that "His only begotten Son" would be the expression of all the facets of His person. So, He arranged for the Son to be able to handle the administration of His authority and power as well as to speak for Him in all things.

Having qualified the Son, He presented Jesus as His exclusive representation. "In the past God spoke to our ancestors through the prophets at many times and in various ways, but in these last days he has spoken to us by his Son…."[219] "God was reconciling the world to himself in Christ, not counting people's sins against them."[220] By remaining in the Father, the Father would put on display all His authority and power through the Son, and the Son may claim the legitimacy of being the extension of the person of His Father. Therefore, although He has a distinct existence, His purpose remained that of His Father. The fulfillment of His Father's purpose reaches its unique apogee in this Son of Promise as was foreordained.

Jesus could, therefore, say that the works He did were not His own, and He only did what He saw His Father doing, because "…the Son can do nothing by himself…."[221] He remained in the Father inasmuch as no aspect of His life was conducted independently of His Father. With this being the clarity of Jesus' understanding, it is not difficult to understand why His being would be so traumatized and He would cry, "…My God, my God, why have you forsaken me?"[222] Although His Spirit knew that He took the place of man and bore the reality of separation from the Father, initiated by Adam, His righteous soul was surprised by the stark reality of that separation, because even in His soul He was never separated from God but always remained in the Father.

The picture that Jesus' life presents of the relationship between the Father and the Son is one that cannot be severed. Jesus, the Son, is consciously aware that His destiny was foreordained by the Father from the foundations of the world, and He consistently chose to embrace that destiny even from the earliest days of His training. The adversities that attend Him from early on are purposefully aligned to results that were necessary to prepare His path. He trusts the Father who arranges these circumstances that shape the path along which His destiny emerges. His trust of the Father permits Him to adopt the Father's choices as His own, and He is, therefore, credited with the same character as that of His Father. The Father, having chosen the destiny of the Son, together with all of the related circumstances, engages the Son in profound fellowship. Over time He imparts to the Son all of the required wisdom, knowledge, understanding, council, and power required to walk in and to complete His destiny. He presents the Son and shows Himself to the world in the most complete expression of His nature that man could behold. This divine reality defines the relationship between Jesus and God and is the archetype for the restored relationship between God and man.

My Father! My Father!

CHAPTER 12

Turning the Heart of the Fathers to the Children

THE SPIRIT OF ELIJAH

The relationship between God the Father and Jesus Christ the Son is the standard order for the restoration of God's house.[223] In the House of God, Jesus is "the firstborn among many brothers and sisters."[224] The prophecy regarding the restoration of God's House at the end of the age is contained within the understanding of the restoration of the relationship of fathers and sons. However, the intention of God is not focused upon the restoration of natural fathers and sons, but instead upon that of spiritual fathers and spiritual sons.

God planned that the arrangement of His spiritual house should be done around this central concept of spiritual fathers and spiritual sons. This concept is carried over from the final prophecy of the Old Testament: "Behold, I will send you Elijah the prophet before the coming of the great and dreadful day of the LORD: And he shall turn the heart of the fathers to the children, and the heart of the children to their fathers, lest I come and smite the earth with a curse."[225] Jesus spoke of this prophecy early in His ministry to define the role of John the Baptist, "if you are willing to accept it, he is the Elijah who was to come."[226] Jesus conditioned the fulfillment of the prophecy to that generation on their acceptance of it—though the prophecy itself was being fulfilled. Indeed, John the Baptist was the spirit of Elijah who was promised.

However, that generation did not benefit from the fulfillment of the prophecy within their day. Other generations who would receive the sign of John the Baptist would understand the significance of the relationship between Jesus and John, heralding the beginning of the restoration of the House of God through the restoration of spiritual fathers and sons. The key to the revelation of the order of fathers and sons, as the basis of the arrangement of the House of God, lies in the understanding of the spirit of Elijah.

The great archangel Gabriel, known for bringing a word directly from God to the earth to effect monumental changes in the flow of human history, prophesied to the father of John the Baptist,

> *Many of the people of Israel will he bring back to the Lord their God. And he will go on before the Lord, in the spirit and power of Elijah, to turn the hearts of the fathers to their children and the disobedient to the wisdom of the righteous— to make ready a people prepared for the Lord.*[227]

John was the spirit of Elijah that preceded Jesus in order to announce Him as the one with the authority to restore the House of God. Jesus would replace the culture of the fatherless with that of a son and would heal the breach between God and man that existed since Adam. He was the scion of the House of God who would restore the glory of a holy people.

The key to this understanding of Jesus is the story of the great prophet Elijah and his servant and understudy, Elisha. Elisha, like Elijah, was a prophet and would become the successor of Elijah. As the time of Elijah's death drew near, he asked Elisha, "Tell me, what can I do for you before I am taken from you?" Elisha responded, "Let me inherit a double portion of your spirit." Elijah said, "You have asked a difficult thing...yet if you see me when I am taken from you, it will be yours—otherwise not."

> *As they were walking along and talking together, suddenly a chariot of fire and horses of fire appeared and separated the two of them, and Elijah went up to heaven in a whirlwind. Elisha saw this and cried out, "My father! My father! The chariots and horsemen of Israel!" And Elisha saw him no more. Then he took hold of his own clothes and tore them apart.*
>
> *He picked up the cloak that had fallen from Elijah and went back and stood on the bank of the Jordan. Then he took the cloak that had fallen from him and struck the water with it. "Where now is the LORD, the God of Elijah?" he asked. When he struck the water, it divided to the right and to the left, and he crossed over."*[228]

The double portion for which Elisha petitioned, and which he received, refers to the portion of a father's estate reserved typically for the firstborn son. By Elijah's own reckoning, Elisha's request for a double portion of his spirit was an unusual and difficult one. The double portion usually concerned the inheritance of money, servants, land, livestock, and other property sufficient to establish and maintain the family of the inheritor and to carry on the function of the house of his forefathers into the next generation. Therefore, the double portion was given to the heir whose character and conduct embodied the purpose for the existence of the family.

Spiritually, the designation of one who inherits from a father is based upon a connection or relationship distinct from a biological one. This is shown by example in the prophetic designation of Judah's tribe as the inheritors of the promise given to Abraham. Similarly, David received the anointing as the first king to come from the line of Judah, notwithstanding his position in his natural family: he was the youngest of his father, Jesse's, sons and the last to be presented to the prophet Samuel who had come to Jesse's house at God's instruction to select and anoint the king of Israel.[229]

God chose David as the king from whose lineage Christ would come, because David was a man after God's own heart.[230]

The concept of the double portion is intertwined with the perpetuation of a house. The double portion concept refers to the son whose character is most closely aligned to the purpose for which the house of his father exists. Every house is established according to a promise from God. At the time the promise is given, it is clear that its fulfillment is to be accomplished over many generations. The Son of Promise is a designation that was usually reserved for the person in whose lifetime the promise was meant to be completely fulfilled. The house was maintained through succeeding generations through the bestowing of the double portion upon the son of the house who, in his generation, manifested the character most closely aligned to the spirit of the promise.

When Jesus came to fulfill the promise given to Abraham, He was the recipient of this double portion. His double portion was the anointing required to break the hold of the culture of the orphan upon humankind and to model the culture of the son. John the Baptist was sent to announce Jesus as the pattern Son to restore the Father's House. God established the prophetic sign of this occurrence at the close of the Old Testament and opens the New Testament by introducing Jesus as His Son.

Elijah functions in a similar capacity in his relationship to Elisha. Elijah was the spiritual father of Elisha; he was not his natural father. So, the inheritance Elisha asked for was not material, but spiritual. He requested "a double portion" of Elijah's spirit. Elisha was, therefore, asking for the portion of a firstborn to carry on the purpose for which Elijah himself had been called as a prophet.

As Elijah is a type of John the Baptist, announcing Elisha as the one with the double portion, so Elisha is a type of Christ who possesses the double portion. The spirit of Elijah, therefore, is the first one to take up the role of the herald to the one with the double portion. That role is reprised by John the Baptist in regard to Christ. When asked about himself, "John replied in the words of

Isaiah the prophet, 'I am the voice of one calling in the wilderness,
"Make straight the way for the Lord.""""[231]

> *The next day, John saw Jesus coming toward him and said,*
> *"Look, the Lamb of God, who takes away the sin of the*
> *world! This is the one I meant when I said, 'A man who*
> *comes after me has surpassed me because he was before me.'*
> *I myself did not know him, but the reason I came baptizing*
> *with water was that he might be revealed to Israel."*
>
> *Then John gave this testimony: "I saw the Spirit come*
> *down from heaven as a dove and remain on him. I would*
> *not have known him, except that the one who sent me to*
> *baptize with water told me, 'The man on whom you see the*
> *Spirit come down and remain is he who will baptize with the*
> *Holy Spirit.' I have seen and I testify that this is the Son of*
> *God."*[232]

John perfectly fulfills the role prophesied for the one who would
come in the spirit of Elijah as the reliable witness to identify the
one sent from God to restore the order of His house.

MY FATHER! MY FATHER!

Elisha's cry of *"My Father, My Father!"* was in recognition that
Elijah was his spiritual father. Elisha had followed Elijah and
observed his way of life for a sufficiently long period of time for
this relationship to have been formed.

When one is born again, he is born into the family of God as
a son. However, the culture of his soul is still intact, and although
he has been spiritually reconciled, he naturally understands the
relationship through the culture of an orphan. He has been re-
patriated to God the Father and has access to the resources of
the great House of God. Yet, he still views himself through the
filters of his native culture. In order for him to transition to the
culture of a son, he must be tutored and disciplined in the culture
of heaven. This task is assigned to a spiritual father.

The roles of the spiritual father and the spiritual son are based on the relationship between God the Father and Jesus Christ the Son. This relationship is the only way to supplant the culture of the orphan with that of a son. Absent this training, a person born again inevitably will continue to function in his native culture of fallenness, because the soul must be brought back to its place of subservience to the spirit. The culture that is native to the spirit must be modeled so that the son can practice it. The spiritual father is, therefore, one whom God has set in the life of a son to watch over his soul.[233] Thus, the spiritual father is required to give an account to God regarding the spiritual son. A spiritual father must be someone who is mature enough to be given as a gift to a spiritual son to reveal the nature of God the Father.

Since God Himself established the arrangement of father and son, He also empowers it to work successfully. God arranges for a spiritual son whose destiny requires the participation of a spiritual father possessed of specific qualities necessary for the training, care, and development of that son. For his part, God has worked in the spiritual father over a considerable period of time to produce accurate reflections of the nature of God in that father. He has gone through all the stages though which the son will progress, and has been matured, having learned obedience by the things he has suffered. It is God's grace to give a father who is mature in the ways of God to instruct, train, and discipline a son who needs exactly that kind of supervision and oversight.

God places both the father and the son in this relationship and confirms to each independently His selection, so that nothing is arranged by force or convenience.

The House of God functions organically, since it is a family and not an institution. The spiritual son possesses a destiny that is a continuation of the vision given to the spiritual father. However, the spiritual father is very clear that the vision he received is greater than can be fulfilled in his own life and requires the vision of his spiritual son to be carried on to the next generation. A true spiritual vision can only be partially fulfilled within a single lifetime.[234]

140

Yet, a father recognizes that the continuing unfolding of the vision may only be accomplished in succeeding generations through the endowments of God's grace and anointing, given uniquely to individuals in those periods of time. Even if the father has a general outline of how God may accomplish the promise in succeeding generations, he recognizes that there are far too many gaps in his understanding to permit him to ordain the course of future generations.

Like God Himself, a spiritual father must practice the humility of having the vision he was given pass into the hands of succeeding generations and permit them to put on display the fulfillment that defines the promise that was given to him. The promise Abraham received as the father was fully interpreted through Christ, and even the relationship between God and Abraham was meant to be understood through the administration of Jesus.

THE EVERLASTING FATHER

Jesus is the reliable and faithful witness of God the Father. One of the titles of Jesus is the "Everlasting Father."[235] He came to the earth with the specific intent of revealing God the Father, with whose ways He was completely familiar. On the earth, He was the spiritual father to the twelve disciples and showed them the exact nature of the Father in Heaven. Because He so fully and accurately embodied that role, He gave form to the heavenly title, "Everlasting Father."

Like the relationship between God the Father and Jesus the Son, a spiritual relationship is built upon a fundamental trust of the spiritual father by the son and a profound love of the son by the father. The son trusts the motives of his father, whereas the father always acts for the benefit of the son. The mature father is himself a source for the radiation of God the Father's glory and a mature representation of the Father's being. He is, therefore, a competent tutor and governor to that son of God assigned to him to be matriculated through the stages of sonship from infancy to maturity. In this way, a son is able to navigate the difficult path from orphan

141

to become a mature son of God and to take up his inheritance and destiny in the House of God.

The power of this arrangement presents an eternal reality that is undeniable. In present human society, completely defined by the orphan culture, a father who acts for the benefit of a natural child is an anomaly. But, a spiritual father with no biological relationship to a spiritual son who consistently acts for the son's good, presents to the world a relationship in which all of the hostilities driving human beings are obliterated, and a picture of divine intentions is revealed again upon the earth.

In the great House of God, people of all different races, socioeconomic classes, ethnic backgrounds, and gender can be assembled in spiritual families, households, and ultimately into an entire nation, which will have succeeded in eradicating all forms of human competition and division. The central idea around which such a nation will be assembled is the principle of a spiritual father and son. On the earth, this principle is a type and a shadow of the reality of the order that is in heaven itself; the Father and the Son seated upon the throne of God. It will be on the earth as it is in heaven.

CHAPTER 13

Call No Man Upon the Earth Your Father

At the center of the relationship between God and man is the Father. Human identity, purpose, and destiny are intimately tied to an understanding of father. In establishing this relationship as the keystone, it is God's purpose that the order of heaven to be replicated on the earth in the House of God is unmistakably patriarchal.[236]

The orphan culture in present society opposes the idea of a patriarchal order with inflamed passion and a harsh criticism of fathers. To a minority of the total human population, "father" evokes the deepest sense of satisfaction and well-being. However, to most, "father" evokes emotions that range from fear to revulsion. The culture of the orphan typically responds with overwhelming negativity to the term "father."

Although large numbers of people are content to forge a life devoid of any reference to "father," the relationship to a father remains the unresolved conflict at the base of most people's lives. As discussed in the earlier chapters of this book, the failure of fathers has been both personal and systemic in the chronicle of the evolution of the culture of orphans from its inception in the Garden of Eden to its current manifestations. Because there has been no clear possibility of resolving this emotional conflict, people make great efforts to avoid discussion or even mention of the issue.

Accordingly, society generally has cultivated a preference for language that supports this pattern of avoidance. This preference is manifested in interpretations of Scripture that attempt to find security and well-being apart from the order of fathers and sons. Most commonly, those opposed to a patriarchal order will cite Jesus' statement, "do not call anyone on earth 'father,' for you have one Father, and he is in heaven,"[237] to support an idea that the only proper usage of the term "father" is one directed toward God. Any other usage is contrary to the words of Jesus and places a person into a position meant exclusively for God. Typically, following this concept is an argument suggesting that the only order or authority to which one should ever submit is God, directly. This has become many people's personal interpretation of the Bible, or at most, a historical point of view to which they accord the status of orthodoxy.

However, a cursory consideration of Scripture reveals the untenable nature of this point of view, particularly considering the writings from the early church apostles. Paul describes his relationship to the believers in Corinth, and to Timothy, as follows:

> *I am writing this not to shame you but to warn you as my dear children. Even if you had ten thousand guardians in Christ, you do not have many fathers, for in Christ Jesus I became your father through the gospel. Therefore I urge you to imitate me. For this reason I have sent to you Timothy, my son whom I love, who is faithful in the Lord. He will remind you of my way of life in Christ Jesus, which agrees with what I teach everywhere in every church.*[238]

Paul identifies himself as the father to the Corinthians and identifies Timothy as his son. He further claims that this relationship exists "in Christ," and is consistent with what he teaches everywhere among the believers. Because Timothy was his spiritual son, Paul could send him as a representative to the Corinthians. Timothy was raised in and familiar with Paul's ways and could, therefore, put the church in Corinth in remembrance of Paul's "Christ-centered life." Paul understood his role as the father to the Corinthian believers and to Timothy to have been ordained by Christ, and his role as father was foundational to his teachings everywhere he preached.

Not only did Paul embrace and advocate this form of order, but in dealing with the Corinthians he actively asserted his fatherly responsibility to confront them with their need for discipline. He provided Timothy as an interim solution, but indicated that he would come to them at a later time to bring correction to them in the full order of what was needed at that time, saying:

> *Some of you have become arrogant, as if I were not coming to you. But I will come to you very soon, if the Lord is willing, and then I will find out not only how these arrogant people are talking, but what power they have. For the kingdom of God is not a matter of talk but of power. What do you prefer? Shall I come to you with a rod of discipline, or shall I come in love and with a gentle spirit?* [239]

This letter shows clearly that Paul was the father to the Corinthians.

In both name and function, the early Church was based on the relationship between individuals as fathers and sons. In addition to referring to Timothy on several other occasions as his son,[240] Paul also referred to Titus and Onesimus as sons,[241] and he functioned as their father. To Titus, Paul wrote, "To Titus, my true son in our common faith…. The reason I left you in Crete was that you might put in order what was left unfinished and appoint elders in every town, as I directed you,"[242] showing that Titus represented Paul and Paul instructed him as a father. Similarly, Paul appealed for Onesimus' provision and treated him as a son, writing:

> *It is as none other than Paul—an old man and now also a prisoner of Christ Jesus—that I appeal to you for my son Onesimus, who became my son while I was in chains. Formerly he*

was useless to you, but now he has become useful both to you and to me. I am sending him—who is my very heart—back to you.[243]

Peter also refers to John Mark as his son,[244] and John frequently referred to groups of believers as his "children."[245]

There is no conflict in Scripture between Jesus' instruction "do not call anyone on earth 'father,'" and the words of Paul, Peter, and John. The explanation is quite simple. Most languages ascribe multiple meanings to a single word and define the particular meaning by the context of usage and one's familiarity with the different ways in which that term may be properly used. For example, an English speaker would understand that there are many different usages of the word "world." If a person says, "I have been traveling in the world," he would intend a different meaning than if he were to say, "My friend, an abstract thinker, lives in his own world." The first statement uses the term "world" geographically, indicating that the speaker has been traveling from country to country, while the latter statement's usage speaks of an intellectual construct regarding the friend's interests and activities.

Accordingly, it is easy to understand that when the apostle John says, "for God so loved the world,"[246] he is referring to a different world than the one he has in mind when he says, "Do not love the world or anything in the world. If anyone loves the world, the love of the Father is not in him."[247] Although he uses the same term for world in both references, he means two completely different things. One refers to humanity, while the other refers to the systems that Satan has created to compete with the Kingdom of God. Both instances properly use the term "world," but the worlds that they refer to are completely opposed to each other.

Similarly, the noted usages of "father" by Jesus and Paul denote different usages and meanings of the same word. There is no contradiction, for example, in referring to a natural father as a "father," and God as "our Father in heaven." It is possible to be born of both fathers, since one is a natural birth, while the other is spiritual.[248]

SPIRITUAL FATHERS

There are nine distinct usages of the word "father" through-out the Scriptures. Jewish persons may refer to Abraham, Isaac, and Jacob as their fathers, since they are their ancient progenitors. Jesus' statement referred to a particular usage, namely that God is the Father of our spirits if we are born again of the Holy Spirit. Paul clearly understood this when he wrote:

> *And if the Spirit of [H]im who raised Jesus from the dead is living in you, [H]e who raised Christ from the dead will also give life to your mortal bodies because of [H]is Spirit who lives in you. …The Spirit you received does not make you slaves, so that you live in fear again; rather, the Spirit you received brought about your adoption to sonship. And by him we cry, "Abba, Father." The Spirit himself testifies with our spirit that we are God's children.*[249]

Paul clearly understood that when we are born again, our spirits become preeminent over our souls and we become new creations, although we remain housed in the same bodies. Since being born again is the restoration of the proper order of spirit and soul within man, God begins to speak again to our spirits as He previously did with Adam in the Garden. He becomes "the Father of our spirits,"[250] inasmuch as we are born again through the work of the Spirit of our Father.

As spiritual beings, we derive our existence and identity from God our Father in contrast to only being born of our natural fathers. It must be noted, however, that the only one who may properly call God "Father" is one born again of His Spirit, since it is the Spirit Himself who testifies with our spirits that we are God's children. It would be inappropriate to refer to anyone else as the one from whom we have derived our spiritual existence.

A spiritual father is God's manner of providing a representation of Himself to His children to bring them to their full maturity. God intends that this order be accorded the honor and respect that reflects the importance He has attached to it. Clearly, Paul recognized that God arranged the order of His House to reflect this heavenly reality on the earth and to restore the culture of heaven to humankind. Regarding the purpose of his role as a father, Paul later writes to the Corinthians, "I am jealous for you with a godly jealousy. I promised you to one husband, to Christ, so that I might present you as a pure virgin to him."[251] He also wrote to the Galatians, "My dear children, for whom I am again in the pains of childbirth until Christ is formed in you, how I wish I could be with you now and change my tone, because I am perplexed about you!"[252] Paul understood his role as one assigned by God to produce mature sons to God. He was the one through whom they received the gospel of Christ, so he fathered them in the faith, and assumed an ongoing responsibility for their growth and maturity.

Similarly, Jesus gave an account for the Twelve that God had given to Him, saying, "I have revealed you to those whom you gave me out of the world. They were yours; you gave them to me and they have obeyed your word," and "I have made you known to them, and will continue to make you known in order that the love you have for me may be in them and that I myself may be in them."[253] Both Jesus and Paul understood that God cares for His children in the world by assigning them to specific fathers who are assigned the responsibility of bringing them to maturity.[254]

The twin factors of the culture of the orphan and the historic abuse and neglect of fathers have created a climate of hostility toward the order of God for the arrangement of His House. Any conception of Scripture that supports and even legitimizes the climate of hostility toward the order of God is erroneous.

God fully intends to restore the order of fathers and sons to His House and to structure a governmental form that models that reality. The purpose of this form is to benefit the sons by transforming their culture through the functioning reality of spiritual fathers who effectively model the character of God the Father. The restoration of heavenly culture is the necessary foundation upon which sons are brought to maturity. Through mature sons, God is pleased to offer His rule as an alternative to the slavery inherent in the kingdom of Satan. God destroys the appeal of this kingdom through the righteous alternative of His mature children.

His House is designed to receive all those escaping the darkness of Satan's kingdom and the blinding effect of the orphan culture on the vision of man. By its order, the House of God reconnects orphans to a father, restoring their destiny and establishing them with a continuity of purpose trans-generationally.

The order of the arrangement of the House of God is the context in which the authority of Christ is received in the earth. The functioning of the Kingdom of God is the governmental basis of support for the entire structure of life that models the order of heaven in the earth. The arrangement of the House of God is designed to reconnect man to God, restore his authority to function, and reinstall him in his destiny.[255]

My Father! My Father!

$\mathcal{T}$he Arrangement of the House of God

ORIGINAL AND DELEGATED AUTHORITY

The House of God is established on the authority of God Himself. He gave that authority to Jesus as an original and exclusive grant.[256] With the vesting of that authority, Jesus became the undisputed King of heaven and earth. His claim is plenary and establishes an absolute preemption against all other claims to authority. It inheres to Him, and He can neither be divested of it nor can He ever alienate it. God would never take it from Him since God swore an oath to establish Jesus as the scion of His House. Therefore, no one else may claim original authority in heaven or on earth.

Jesus' advent into the world took place pursuant to this oath.[257] During His life on the earth, God announced Jesus' birth by angels and introduced Him at the beginning of His ministry as His Son, attesting to Jesus' suitability to represent God, by the sign of the Holy Spirit descending on Him and the voice of God speaking from heaven. Finally, giving Him all authority in heaven and on earth, God raised Him from the dead, and in the plain sight of a crowd of witnesses, Jesus ascended to heaven.

The first message Jesus' disciples preached was on the Day of Pentecost, ten days after His ascension into heaven. Peter used the occasion to announce to the Jewish nation that Jesus was the

King whose advent had been long prophesied. Peter was part of a company of twelve witnesses necessary under the legal requirements of the day to establish proof of an event. They offered the eyewitness testimony that Jesus was resurrected and ascended to heaven, fulfilling the standards for identifying the King that were established by King David.[258]

Whoever claims to have authority in the domains of heaven and earth must show a legitimate connection to Jesus' plenary authority, because one may only claim such authority as a delegate of Christ. From His place at the right hand of the Father, Jesus directs the use of His authority on the earth in all of its manifestations. He designated the Holy Spirit as His prime delegate and committed to the Spirit His authority to establish His Kingdom on earth. The authority of Jesus came to earth when the blessed Holy Spirit was "pour[ed] out" on all people.[259]

The Holy Spirit arranges all of the relationships that form the House of God and controls how they function. He is also present in each person who is part of the House of God. It is the central presence of the Holy Spirit that permits the alignment of the sons of God into the collective family. If God could not fellowship with the spirit of an individual, He could not assert the necessary influence over the person's character or actions. This fellowship functions on the basis of one's relationship to God as Father, "For those who are led by the Spirit of God are the children of God."[260]

THE HOLY SPIRIT

Since no institution has a living spirit with whom the Holy Spirit may fellowship, it is impossible for the Holy Spirit to bring order and discipline to any institution. Institutions are merely fictional representations of an actual corpus, existing only as long as they are empowered by a group or government. The authority of an institution is rooted in the goals of the empowering body, not in a relationship to God. It is impossible for any institution to claim a relationship with the Holy Spirit. Yet, the Holy Spirit operates through His relationship with a human spirit. Without the prerequisite relationship with Christ's delegate, the Holy Spirit, no person or institution may claim the authority of Christ, since the Holy Spirit is the only means He appointed for the administration of His power. All institutions, therefore, are outside the flow of the delegated authority of Christ.

The Holy Spirit empowers the unique spirit of an individual. During a person's life, his spirit accommodates the Spirit of God, which makes him into a son who represents the Father in His rule. A claim that a grant of authority from Jesus to a particular individual may subsequently be conserved in an institution, and further delegated through that institution's administration, ignores the fact that the Holy Spirit continually stewards such a grant of authority by interacting with one's spirit. When the person who received the grant of authority dies, the purpose for his unique spirit ends, and the power granted to him lapses; his destiny is complete. The Holy Spirit does not continue to steward the grant of authority in an institution. Institutions can never accommodate the Spirit of God since they do not exist as living beings with spirits.

The power of Christ is delegated to enable persons under the control of the spirit to fulfill the destiny God appointed for them. Any attempt to represent the power of Jesus Christ other than through the Holy Spirit constitutes a challenge to the place of the Holy Spirit and to the very authority of Christ, of which He is the exclusive delegate.

THE SPIRIT ARRANGES THE HOUSE

The Holy Spirit assigns the fathers to the sons and the sons to the fathers, matching the fathers' abilities to the sons' unique needs. The fathers are judged to be worthy of being fathers by reason of their demonstrated maturity. The Spirit knows the unique destiny of every son, because He is familiar with the intent in the mind of God behind the creation of each person.

"What no eye has seen, what no ear has heard, and what no human mind has conceived"—the things God has prepared

> *for those who love him—these are the things God has re-*
> *vealed to us by his Spirit. The Spirit searches all things, even*
> *the deep things of God.*[261]

The Holy Spirit holds the fathers accountable for the proper treat-
ment of the sons, and requires the sons to acknowledge His authority in the fathers and to be accountable to them. The arrangement
of the relationship is designed with the good of the sons in mind.
The order established by the Holy Spirit is designed to mature the
sons as well as to make the entire House of God the instrument by
which God accomplishes His eternal purpose on earth.

The House of God is not an end within itself, but a means to
an end. As a son of God increases in maturity, God endows him
with greater knowledge of his destiny and an increased measure
of power and authority sufficient to fulfill the increment of his
destiny entrusted to him at that time. The Holy Spirit then integrates
each son's destiny into the unfolding manifestation of God's corporate purpose. Just as Jesus revealed the nature of the Father and the
Father glorified the son, so also the corporate Christ reveals the glory
of the Father. The Holy Spirit arranges the corporate Christ so that
each son is also revealed, in the level of his maturity, as the fullness
of Christ is put on display:

> *Since, then, you have been raised with Christ, set your hearts*
> *on things above, where Christ is seated at the right hand of*
> *God. Set your minds on things above, not on earthly things.*
> *For you died, and your life is now hidden with Christ in God.*
> *When Christ, who is your life, appears, then you also will*
> *appear with him in glory.*[262]

All the sons, properly arranged as the House of God and functioning by the authority of Christ, establish on earth a picture of the
order of God in heaven. This alternative way of life will stand in
stark contrast to the form of life that has been on the earth since
the fall of man, in which Satan's influence has been compounded

and has had the long-term effect of blinding man to the reality of the love of God.

The restoration of the order of the House of God is designed to put on display the complete picture of the nature of God as revealed through Christ during His time upon the earth. God's intent is to reconcile humankind to Himself through the corporate Christ.[263]

A Copy and Shadow of What is in Heaven

God planned to bring realities that have previously existed in heaven into the earth in the same manner in which they exist in heaven.[264] These realities are for the benefit of all humankind, but particularly that portion of His house that lives upon the earth.[265] The simultaneous coexistence of these heavenly things in both realms is meant to harmonize the standards of earth to those of heaven. This was always part of the overall plan of God to redeem humankind to His original intent for them.

The House of God on the earth is the enclave through which God introduces the realities of heavenly standards into the earth. Within the venue of earth, the House of God is designed to put heavenly realities on display. The environment within this enclave is simultaneously compatible to heaven's mandates while foreign to the normal environment of earth. Although it is meant to be beneficial to humankind, its strangeness to the culture of earth often causes it to be viewed with suspicion, misunderstanding, and even hostility.

Historically, God has arranged types and shadows of these heavenly realities among His people in advance of the coming of the realities to remind His people of the promises that He has made that would progressively be fulfilled as the realities transitioned into the earth from heaven. These types and shadows are sent in order to sensitize their culture and predispose their souls to receive the heavenly impartations. At such times, the people of God who walk in the understanding provided by types and shadows are lights to the nations in which they are placed.

The existence of a shadow of a heavenly thing presumes that the thing itself has not yet transitioned to earth. For example, "[The Levitical Priests] served at a sanctuary that is a copy and shadow of what is in heaven....But in fact the ministry Jesus has received is as superior to theirs as the covenant of which he is mediator is superior to the old one, since the new covenant is established on better promises."[266] Paul writes in Hebrews 8 that by calling the covenant brought by Jesus "new," the old covenant served by the Levitical priesthood was made "obsolete; and what is obsolete and outdated will soon disappear."[267] As long as the copy remained, it was certain that the reality had not yet appeared.

> *The Holy Spirit was showing by this that the way into the Most Holy Place had not yet been disclosed as long as the first tabernacle was still functioning. ...But when Christ came as high priest of the good things that are now already here, he went through the greater and more perfect tabernacle that is not made with human hands, that is to say, is not a part of this creation.*[268]

As long as the copy remains, it is certain that access into the reality has not yet been granted, but when the reality makes its advent, it is supported by the necessary power and authority to enable it to function, and it is attended by the requisite order to accomplish the purposes for which it was designed:

> *It was necessary, then, for the copies of the heavenly things to be purified with these sacrifices, but the heavenly things themselves with better sacrifices than these. For Christ did not enter a sanctuary made with human hands that was only a copy of the true one; he entered heaven itself, now to appear for us in God's presence.*[269]

It is only after this transition has occurred that access into the reality can be granted, and an accompanying duty to enter it is required.

Regarding the House of God itself, it existed previously in type and shadow in Abraham's house. The arrangement of Abraham's house was a copy and shadow of the House of God designed to familiarize the earth with the order of a holy nation. The order of Abraham's house, therefore, is useful to develop the understanding of the revelation of the House of God in the earth.

FROM CHALDEA TO CANAAN

God gave the promise to Abraham that he would be the father of a great nation, through which Christ would eventually be brought into the world. Although God gave the promise to Abraham directly, it was not until four generations later that a sketchy outline of the form of the promise would begin to emerge—it would be forty-two generations from the time of the promise to its ultimate fulfillment. Four generations from the time of the promise, twelve sons were born to Jacob, and a nation began to take shape. These twelve sons would become the patriarchs of the tribes that would form the framework for the future nation. However, it would not be for another four hundred years, when Israel emerged from Egypt, that Moses would arrange them in the form of a nation.

The timing of the Lord is a vital component of His promises. From the time of the issuance of a promise to its fulfillment, many changes are necessary in order for the promise to be fulfilled. Without these changes, the promises either could not be fulfilled or their fulfillment would not be a blessing to those receiving the promise.

In the case of Abraham, the transitions of his people were crucial to the fulfillment of the promise. Abraham began life in Ur of the Chaldees and grew up in a polytheistic society. Although Abraham himself believed in the one true God, he came from a family that had household gods.[270] Knowing this, he would not permit his son Isaac to leave Canaan even to go to find a wife among his kinfolk. Instead, his servant Eleazar was dispatched on the mission.[271] After Abraham had been liberated from the influences of that polytheistic culture, he was unwilling to permit the son of promise to come under that influence. Three generations were required to transition to a monotheistic culture. In the fourth generation, the fathers of the nation were born.

By then, the culture had fully transitioned. The change was evident when Joseph prophesied the resurrection of the nation from Egypt and charged Israel to take his remains back to Canaan for final burial. Even though he could have had one of the most elaborate burial chambers in Egypt because of his exalted status, it was important to him to be identified with the culture of his fathers and their unique promise.

God intended to fulfill the promise to Abraham by bringing the Redeemer into the world through an entire nation, since it would require an entire nation to model the culture that would come with the fulfilling of the promise, displaying a veiled order of heaven. This type and shadow prepared the way for the advent of the House of God, in which the fullness of who Christ is and what He accomplished would be put on display through a holy nation.

The comparison between reality and its antecedent is obvious. Jesus also began to form the holy nation with the twelve men God gave Him. The notable difference between Abraham and Jesus was that, as the living God, Jesus did not require a change in culture, and His disciples could learn the culture of heaven from His perfect presentation of it.

The Old Testament revealed in detail the order of the nation that emerged from Egypt through an incident that occurred shortly after Israel entered the Promised Land. As they came to the first city in Canaan, God required that all the silver and gold and articles of bronze and iron taken from the city of Jericho be devoted to Him and be put into the treasury of the Lord's house.[272] The fact that not everyone complied with this was not discovered immediately. Israel's fighting force anticipated a second miraculous victory over the city of Ai as they moved into position to attack that city.

So confident were they of the outcome, that upon the recommendation of their scouting party, they took only a token force of about three thousand men. They were completely taken by surprise at the ferocity of the defenders and fled in a rout, losing thirty-six members of the attacking party in the skirmish. Joshua, now the leader of Israel since the death of Moses, suffered his first major defeat and was devastated. In his torment and confusion, he tore his clothes and fell facedown to the ground before the Lord and stayed in that position for several hours.[273]

> *The Lord said to Joshua, "Stand up! What are you doing down on your face? Israel has sinned; they have violated my covenant, which I commanded them to keep. They have taken some of the devoted things; they have stolen, they have lied, they have put them with their own possessions. That is why the Israelites cannot stand against their enemies; they turn their backs and run because they have been made liable to destruction. I will not be with you anymore unless you destroy whatever among you is devoted to destruction."*[274]

The Lord then gave Joshua specific instructions as to how to discover the sin among the people, which also reveal the arrangement of this nation. They were to consecrate themselves as they prepared to stand before the Lord the following day.

> *In the morning, present yourselves tribe by tribe. The tribe the LORD chooses shall come forward clan by clan; the clan the LORD chooses shall come forward family by family; and the family the LORD chooses shall come forward man by man. Whoever is caught with the devoted things shall be destroyed by fire, along with all that belongs to him. He has violated the covenant of the LORD and has done an outrageous thing in Israel!*[275]

By these instructions, God revealed how He connected relationships that formed the nation of Israel.

This was God's design for connecting a person to an entire

nation, and the nation to the person. The prosperity and well-being of the whole nation determined the condition of the individual, and the actions of the individual could determine what happened to the entire nation: "But the Israelites were unfaithful in regard to the devoted things; Achan son of Karmi, the son of Zimri, the son of Zerah, of the tribe of Judah, took some of them. So the Lord's anger burned against Israel."[276] Although Achan acted alone, his actions were attributed to all of Israel, and the attendant consequences were borne by the entire nation. When God addressed the matter to Joshua, he did not refer to the sin of Achan, but to the sin of Israel. The entire nation was contaminated by the sin of one man, and all suffered the consequences equally.

A further examination of the story of Achan yields valuable insights into how God structured the nation of Israel as a type and shadow of His spiritual house:

> *Early the next morning Joshua had Israel come forward by tribes, and Judah was chosen. The clans of Judah came forward, and the Zerahites were chosen. He had the clan of the Zerahites come forward by families, and Zimri was chosen. Joshua had his family come forward man by man, and Achan son of Karmi, the son of Zimri, the son of Zerah, of the tribe of Judah, was chosen.*[277]

Upon the discovery that Israel's troubles were related to the activities of Achan, he was set before the entire nation and confessed his wrongdoing. He had taken for himself certain quantities of gold and silver together with a fine garment of Babylonian origin. These he had hidden under the main pole in his tent.[278]

The consequences that followed are stunning. Achan, his sons and daughters, together with his livestock and all of his other goods and possessions, were taken to the valley of Achor. "…Then all Israel stoned him, and after they had stoned the rest, they burned them. Over Achan they heaped up a large pile of rocks, which remains to this day…."[279] His immediate family was killed with him, and his lineage was cut off from Israel. The consequences of his actions were as extreme for him personally as they were for the nation of Israel. Joshua and the army lost the battle with Ai and suffered thirty-six casualties. Achan lost his life and those of his sons and daughters, effectively obliterating his lineage from Israel.

FAMILIES AND HOUSEHOLDS

The story of Achan reveals a distinct societal order. At the first level of this order was the family. Achan had his own family, comprising his sons and daughters. He was selected from among the children of his father, Karmi, who in turn was selected from among the sons of his father, Zimri. It is not known whether Achan's father and grandfather were alive, but he was from among the families that came from the line of Zimri. Because Achan himself had a family, the reference to the family of his grandfather Zimri is a reference to the collection of families known as a household.

When the Scriptures refer to the family of Zimri, the implication is that all the families out of his line were selected from among the clan of the Zerahites. Since a person's immediate family is part of an ancestral family, it is appropriate to refer to both as a family. However, the term "household" is appropriate when it is necessary to distinguish between an immediate family and a group of families together. In this context, the household would refer to a unit comprising many families, whereas a family would refer to the individual family unit, such as "Achan…his sons and daughters…."[280] Whereas, the word household (bayith) may refer to a building like a fortress or a dungeon, or even a facility that houses a family, its particular application is to a family that may comprise several families.[281]

Abraham's household, then, comprised many families. As head of this household, Abraham was head over not just his immediate family, but of his kinsmen. Accordingly, when word came to Abraham that his nephew Lot had been abducted, "he called out the three hundred eighteen trained men born in his household and went in pursuit," because his nephew Lot was part of his household.[282] Lot was of the household of Abram before he separated his family and went out on his own.

In a separate incident, God chose not to keep from Abraham His decision to destroy the city of Sodom where Lot lived with his wife and his two daughters. God decided to tell Abraham what He was about to do, knowing that Abraham would plead with Him not to destroy Lot in the process. The Lord said:

> *Shall I hide from Abraham what I am about to do? Abraham will surely become a great and powerful nation, and all nations on earth will be blessed through him. For I have chosen him, so that he will direct his children and his household after him to keep the way of the LORD by doing what is right and just, so that the LORD will bring about for Abraham what he has promised him.*[283]

God's plan for Abraham was to train him to faithfully obey the ways of God. He was also instructed to direct his children to observe carefully and to incorporate as the central tenet of their family life the will of God from one generation to another. The result would be that, long after Abraham had died, his household would mature into a holy nation.

God established the family as the environment in which the children would be introduced to the culture of heaven, through the training and instructions of their fathers. The principal duties of the father were to instill obedience and reverence for the commandments and decrees of God and to supervise the disciplining and training of each child. God specifically held the father accountable for these results.

> *These are the commands, decrees and laws the LORD your God directed me to teach you to observe in the land that you are crossing the Jordan to possess, so that you, your children and their children after them may fear the LORD your God as long as you live by keeping all his decrees and commands*

that I give you, and so that you may enjoy long life. ...These
commandments that I give you today are to be upon your
hearts. Impress them on your children. Talk about them
when you sit at home and when you walk along the road,
when you lie down and when you get up. Tie them as symbols
on your hands and bind them on your foreheads. Write them
on the doorframes of your houses and on your gates.[284]

Under the tutelage of fathers, children would come to have insight
into the ways of God, and would be afforded appropriate guidance
as they proceeded to walk in this knowledge:

Fix these words of mine in your hearts and minds; tie them
as symbols on your hands and bind them on your foreheads.
Teach them to your children, talking about them when you
sit at home and when you walk along the road, when you lie
down and when you get up. Write them on the doorframes of
your houses and on your gates, so that your days and the days
of your children may be many in the land the LORD swore
to give your ancestors, as many as the days that the heavens
are above the earth.[285]

The duty of a father was to provide continuity of instruction regarding the requirements of the promise that distinguished this
nation among the peoples of the earth. As a nation, they carried
forward the seed of the fulfillment of the promise:

In days to come, when your son asks you, "What does this
mean?" say to him, "With a mighty hand the LORD
brought us out of Egypt, out of the land of slavery. ...
This is why I sacrifice to the LORD the first male offspring
of every womb and redeem each of my firstborn sons." And
it will be like a sign on your hand and a symbol on your
forehead that the LORD brought us out of Egypt with his
mighty hand.[286]

Until the promise was fulfilled through Christ, the nation harbored the necessary duty of maintaining a culture that was conducive to the fulfillment of the promise. This duty was firmly assigned to fathers, and the culture itself was meant to be nurtured and preserved within the family.

DUTIES AND BENEFITS OF BELONGING TO A HOUSEHOLD

In the model of Abraham's house, families are meant to form together into households, and eventually into a nation. The misconduct of an individual could have lethal consequences, not only for his family but also for the household to which the family belonged, and ultimately even for the nation. The place of the family within the household came with both duties and benefits. The individual members of the family are meant to be part of a greater community to which they owed the duty of maintaining the good name and reputation of the family line. Inasmuch as God's promises are to fathers and their generations after them, no one was meant to live and function exclusively as an individual. There was an established sense of accountability not only to one's father and the immediate family but also to that group of families who came from a common ancestor.

There were also numerous benefits to the individual who belonged to a household. In the case of widows and orphans, the household had specific duties to care for them. This culture existed prior to the nation of Israel. Terah, the father of Abram, Nahor, and Haran, left Ur of the Chaldees after his son Haran died. He took with him Abram, his grandson Lot (Haran's son), and his daughter-in-law Sarai and headed out to Canaan. Later, when Terah died, the Lord said to Abram, "'Go from your country, your people and your father's household to the land I will show you.' ...So Abram went, as the LORD had told him; and Lot went with him...."[287] First, Terah assumed responsibility for his grandson Lot, and upon his death, that responsibility was transferred to Abram, his eldest son. Abram was seventy-five years old at the time, and had no children of his own since Sarai was barren. For all intents and purposes, his nephew, Lot, was his heir.

The role of households was critical to the stability of early cities, and fathers of households acted for the benefit of the families under their protection. Because ancient peoples settled in ancestral lands, agriculture and animal husbandry formed significant parts of the economic life of these societies. Over time, cities were formed to facilitate trading and protection. These cities were populated by households. Fathers of households would assemble at the gates of the city to conduct all manner of transactions. The orderliness of their administration was the underlying foundation for the peace and prosperity of the families that made up the city. These cities were part of the inheritance given to a clan.

CLANS, TRIBES, AND A NATION

The households of Zimri were part of the clan of the Zerahites, and the clan of the Zerahites was among the many other clans that formed the tribe of Judah. The nation of Israel itself comprised twelve tribes, among which was the tribe of Judah. Each of the divisions of the nation was designed to perform a particular function intimately associated with the very reason for the existence of the nation.

Each tribe was given an allotment of land as its inheritance. Clans settled in the regions of their tribal land grant, and eventually established cities within these regions. Since tribes and clans, like households, came from a common ancestor, families that were bound together by a common bloodline and a common history populated all the cities within an ancestral land grant. This afforded maximum regional stability and ultimately national stability. It was the foundation of both national identity and prophetic purpose. Although each person was an individual with a unique destiny, everyone was aware of belonging to a greater whole. Personal identity was supported by a greater sense of common history and an inheritance in land. The laws of Israel recognized the importance of maintaining a person's connection to an estate in land.

A prime example is the year of Jubilee, which was designed

to restore families to their connection with their ancestral identity tangibly connected to their ownership of the land. Every fiftieth year, all lands alienated from their original owners through hardships and adversities will return to the direct descendants living at the time.

> *Consecrate the fiftieth year and proclaim liberty throughout the land to all its inhabitants. It shall be a jubilee for you; each of you is to return to your family property and to your own clan. ...In this Year of Jubilee everyone is to return to their own property. If you sell land to any of your own people or buy land from them, do not take advantage of each other. You are to buy from your own people on the basis of the number of years since the Jubilee. ...The land must not be sold permanently, because the land is mine and you reside in my land as foreigners and strangers. ...If anyone among you becomes poor and sells some of their property, their nearest relative is to come and redeem what they have sold.*[288]

Within the Levitical Codex, many regulations provided for the redemption of agricultural land, houses within cities, and even personal service contracts. The laws that governed the repatriation of families to their ancestral estates in land were clearly designed to maintain an ongoing connection to their unique purpose as the descendants of Abraham. They did so by creating and maintaining a culture that held the people together. The order renewed the nation every fiftieth year by resetting the families within their heritage and inheritance.

Even the concept of patriarch was associated with a land grant. Historically, the word "patriarch" referred to both father and ancestral homeland. The term "patria" is derived from that root and commonly refers to the country of one's fathers. When the Lord gave the promise to Abraham, He gave to him and his descendants "...this land, from the Wadi of Egypt to the great river, the Euphrates—the land of the Kenites, Kenizzites,

Kadmonites, Hittites, Perizzites, Rephaites, Amorites, Canaanites, Girgashites and Jebusites."[289] Beginning with Abraham, the promise of the Messiah included the grant of land.

In the time of Joshua, God gave Israel the inheritance in land He had promised to Abraham. Joshua presided over the orderly distribution of it. Each tribe was given its portion with the exception of the tribe of Levi, since they were to serve as priests among the people.[290] Each tribe subdivided its grant among the clans of the tribe, and the households of that clan further divided their allotment among the families of the household. Israel received and occupied the land according to this order.

This order persisted until the time of enslavement in Babylon. When King David established the order of the tabernacle, he arranged the duties by tribes, clans, households, and families.[291] The same order was carried over into Solomon's temple that followed. Centuries later, when Israel was restored to its ancestral homeland after seventy years in captivity in Babylon, both Ezra and Nehemiah, the leaders of Israel at that time, restored the nation by rearranging the returning refugees according to the same ancient order.[292]

This arrangement of a nation preserved in human culture the order that presents heavenly realities. The nation was arranged in this fashion to contain the heavenly order of the Father and Son and to exhibit this heavenly culture among the nations of the world. Since the Father and Son are Spirit, in order to display the full extent of the life in them, an entire nation was required. The love a father has for a son and the trust of a son for the father is the central form of this order. The complete display of all the facets of this central relationship could only be demonstrated in its entirety through a nation.

From the individual person to the entire nation, God intended to infuse this order with the heavenly reality. No order may exist corporately that does not exist individually, since the corporate expression is the summary of what exists in the individual components. If the individual gave honor and respect to God, then the nation would reflect the same reverence; and correspondingly, if the individual did not know God or choose to honor Him, neither would the nation.

SUMMARY OF PURPOSE FOR THE ORDER OF THE HOUSE

In the arrangement of both the natural and spiritual nations, the purpose of the order was the same. At all of the levels of its function, the order was designed to restore man to his Father and to reconnect him to the Father's nature as expressed through the culture of rule. Once this restoration takes place, the next step is to restore him to the status as a son so he may be trained to represent his Father. The final objective of the process is to restore his destiny and to empower him to function within it.

As a consequence of being restored to his Father, he is placed within the family of his Father. This primary step facilitates two important objectives. First, he learns about the nature of the Father; and second, he learns how to relate to others as brothers. In learning about the ways of the Father, he learns how to rule in his sphere of influence for the benefit of others instead of using his authority and influence to provide for and to protect himself. In relating to others as brothers, he learns how his Father sees each son, and he is rescued from a culture of competition and self-centeredness. Eventually, when he is fully mature, he is able to lay down his life for his brothers as his Father would.

When Adam separated himself from his Father, within one generation, the spirit of genocide was introduced to human culture when his son Cain murdered his brother Abel. With the death of Abel, all of the generations that were to be born out of him were extinguished as well. The root of the scourge of genocide is the devaluation of the brother due to a lack of common identity defined by a father. The restoration of the value of the brother is essential to the eradication of the culture of genocide from human society. The spiritual family is vastly superior to the biological family in achieving this result since, within a spiritual family, the peaceful coexistence of races, genders, and social classes as sons to the same spiritual father is an earthly model of a divine concept.

THE SPIRITUAL FAMILY

The spiritual father trains sons individually even though they are part of the overall family, so no one is overlooked or neglected. The instruction is personal as well as general, and relevant instruction is always imparted personally so that the application benefits the son in his present state. In this model, information does not become a substitute for a father, and general meetings do not take the place of the life of a family. The members of the family know each other by the spirit. That is, they are familiar with the spiritual gifts and divine calling of each member of the family and are aware of the level of their maturity and relate to them based on these factors. They routinely update their understanding of the family members to reflect the growth and maturity of each member, so that no one has to fight for his place in the family. The father's role is vital to the confirmation of the growth and progress of each son.

As each son is ready to assume greater measures of rule and influence, the father is typically the first to go ahead of the son and make the way for his advancement to the new levels of authority and responsibility. At the same time, the family affirms his advancement and supports the son as he accedes to his place of greater influence. An inherent value of this culture is the value of the individual to the whole family. The advancement of one means the advancement of all, while the consequence of the misconduct of one attenuates to everyone.[293]

This culture recognizes that individuals are like parts of a body and they exist in a harmonious and symbiotic arrangement. One of the metaphors that describes this arrangement is the Body of Christ.

The greater levels of complexity described by the household, clan, and nation permit the individual to act in pursuit of his destiny in greater fields of endeavor as well as with greater support. His life within a household impacts a city, while his life within a clan affects an entire region, and ultimately his life within a nation affects the nations of the world. The culture rooted in the relationship of a father and son is by definition a trans-generational culture. When this culture is carried forward by means of a holy nation, its effects transform the culture of fatherlessness and are not dissipated over time.

The revelation of a holy nation, together with the order of its arrangement, means that humankind has entered a new season in which this ancient order is being established in a new manifestation on the earth. Human creations that have substituted for this divine imperative are being disrobed of their pretense and shown in all of their nakedness and vulgarity. Human society has already turned away from these aberrations in their search for answers. Among the nations there is a growing, if unidentified, desire for the authentic truth. It is into this environment that God has chosen to insert the current revelation of this truth. He is assembling people from every tribe, language, people, and nation who are earnestly desiring to be part of the heavenly reality—even if they are not clearly aware that this is what they are seeking.

CHAPTER 15

The Nation of Israel and the Early Church

A TYPE AND SHADOW

God intended to present Israel as a holy nation among nations. Israel, however, was never meant to be the complete expression of the reality of a holy nation, but only a type and shadow. Israel itself was a nation based in a common, natural ancestry, whereas the House of God is a spiritual reality, based upon spiritual relationships. All of Israel was related by blood as a single race of people, descended from Abraham, Isaac, and Jacob. The House of God, however, would comprise people of all races, joined together by spirit, to present the full expression of the love between God the Father and Jesus Christ the Son. In this spiritual arrangement, the type and shadow of Abraham's race would be replaced by the Body of Christ, one being natural, the other spiritual.

At Mount Sinai, God revealed to Moses that He intended to make the nation of Israel a type and shadow of the Body of Christ, by designating Israel as a royal priesthood and a holy nation. "'...Although the whole earth is mine, you will be for me a kingdom of priests and a holy nation.' These are the words you are to speak to the Israelites."[294] This result, however, did not come about, because of Israel's fear of God and its subsequent refusal to accept this offer. Instead of going up into the presence of God as a nation, they responded with fear and designated Moses as their

171

representative before God.[295] God responded by giving them the Law instead of this covenant and selecting the tribe from which Moses came to be the priests who would officiate between God and the people, inasmuch as the people chose Moses to be the mediator between themselves and God. Rather than becoming a nation of royal priests, only qualified men from the tribe of Levi were permitted to function as priests.

This particular failing disqualified Israel from becoming a natural picture of the House of God among the nations of their day. Had they accepted God's offer and obeyed God's commands, they would have become the existing order of royal priests among whom the Gentile believers in Christ would have been integrated. The priesthood would never have been changed from the existing order of Melchizedek to the order of Levi.[296] This prior existing order had been around since before Israel's migration to Egypt, and was named for Melchizedek, the priest who served Abraham bread and wine.[297]

The apostle Paul describes this particular incident, which resulted in the Law replacing God's intended covenant with Israel, as the "severity" or "sterness" of God, and warned the Gentiles not to follow this example of unbelief:

> *I am talking to you Gentiles. Inasmuch as I am the apostle to the Gentiles.... For if their rejection is the reconciliation of the world, what will their acceptance be but life from the dead. ...[I]f the root is holy, so are the branches. If some of the branches have been broken off, and you, though a wild olive shoot, have been grafted in among the others and now share in the nourishing sap from the olive root, do not boast over those branches. ...Consider therefore the kindness and sternness of God: sternness to those who fell, but kindness to you, provided that you continue in his kindness. Otherwise you also will be cut off. And if they do not persist in unbelief, they will be grafted in, for God is able to graft them in again.[298]*

The apostle Peter concurred and declared that the Gentiles indeed had succeeded whereas Israel had been rejected because of their unbelief:

> *As you come to him, the living Stone—rejected by men but chosen by God and precious to him—you also, like living stones are being built into a spiritual house to be a holy priesthood, offering spiritual sacrifices acceptable to God through Jesus Christ. …They stumble because they disobey the message—which is also what they were destined for. But you are a chosen people, a royal priesthood, a holy nation, a people belonging to God, that you may declare the praises of him who called you out of darkness into his wonderful light. Once you were not a people, but now you are the people of God; once you had not received mercy, but now you have received mercy.*[299]

God's intended purpose of Israel as a nation was to put them on display as the model of heavenly order and culture among the nations of the earth. Had Israel chosen to accept the beneficial interests of God's promise to Abraham, to which they were the heirs, God would have made them into a kingdom of priests and a holy nation. It is significant to note that they were given this opportunity before the Law was given to them on Mount Sinai.

God's original plan was to make them into a picture of the spiritual house among the nations of the world until the reality of the house had fully migrated from heaven to earth. They would have been the place-holders for the Body of Christ until it subsequently came following the resurrection and ascension of Christ Himself. In anticipation of this destiny, God arranged them relationally by family, household, clan, tribe, and nation to create an organic form to accommodate the substance of being a royal priesthood and a holy nation.

God brought them to Mount Sinai to confirm His intention to fulfill His promise to their forefather Abraham with them. They were the current successors in interest to the precreation covenant, the promise of which had been given, more than four hundred years earlier, to Abraham. God arranged their nation deliberately to accommodate the reality of this promise. It was created this way to nurture a culture compatible with the promise of a Seed arising from this nation to become the fulfillment of the promise. Their refusal to obey God and accept the offer made to them did not nullify God's intention for them, because the promise to Abraham could only be fulfilled through them.

Israel did not become the type and shadow of a holy nation to which God would assemble the people from the nations of humankind, who would be called and chosen to be the Body of Christ. Instead, their value in Scripture as a type and shadow is limited to the manner of their arrangement as a nation, since God arranged them in this way in anticipation of offering them the opportunity to become an expression of the holy nation.

The Law was given to them in lieu of the promise, and it had the effect of making them into a symbol of the reality. "The law is only a shadow of the good things that are coming—not the realities themselves. For this reason it can never, by the same sacrifices repeated endlessly year after year, make perfect those who draw near to worship."[300] In the appointed time, however, the reality appeared as the Body of Christ. It was always God's plan to bring the reality into being, but even when that type and shadow substitutes for the reality, the order inherent in the substitute is designed to acquaint humans with the existence of the reality, and to make them familiar with it.

As part of the employment of this concept, the recitation of the genealogical record of everyone who was introduced in Scripture, including Jesus, is to show the continuity of God's unfolding plan through human personages. The genealogical reports act as an affidavit, certifying the record of God's divine order, inexorably unfolding through the generations of humanity. This is a blatant declaration that there is divine order by which all things are arranged within the physical creation.[301] This repetitive and redundant practice is to alert even the casual observer to the fact that the visible order is a type and shadow of an invisible order that is no less real than the visible order. Familiarity with the visible order is designed to predispose the understanding of humankind to the existence of this spiritual order and to induce reliance upon it as a means of entering into the designated purpose that underlies the known physical order.

THE SPIRITUAL ORDER OF THE HOUSE OF GOD

The obvious distinction between Abraham's house and the House of God is that one is a natural house, and the other one spiritual. While Israel was based upon natural ancestry and common history, the House of God comprises people of all races who have gone through a process of rebirth into one spiritual race:

> *Therefore, remember that formerly you who are Gentiles by birth and called "uncircumcised" by those who call themselves "the circumcision"...remember that at that time you were separate from Christ, excluded from citizenship in Israel and foreigners to the covenants of the promise[.] ...Consequently, you are no longer foreigners and aliens, but fellow citizens with God's people and also members of God's household, built on the foundation of the apostles and prophets, with Christ Jesus himself as the chief cornerstone. In him the whole building is joined together and rises to become a holy temple in the Lord. And in him you too are being built together to become a dwelling in which God lives by his Spirit.*[302]

Israel represents the arrangement of the natural house while the spiritual house is the Body of Christ.

In a holy race, composed of Jews and Gentiles alike, natural ancestry is replaced by a spiritual fatherhood. The apostle Paul, in the first of his two letters to the Corinthian church, declares to them his fatherly status together with his intentions to actually discipline them, as any responsible father would, considering their existing state of rebellion against his previous instructions, writing:

> *I am writing this not to shame you but to warn you as my dear children. Even if you had ten thousand guardians in Christ, you do not have many fathers, for in Christ Jesus I became your father through the gospel. Therefore I urge you to imitate me. For this reason I have sent to you Timothy, my son whom I love, who is faithful in the Lord. He will remind you of my way of life in Christ Jesus, which agrees with what I teach everywhere in every church. …What do you prefer? Shall I come to you with a rod of discipline, or shall I come in love and with a gentle spirit?*[303]

Like Abraham, Paul understood that there is an existing promise that is being fulfilled in order to reveal the Christ. For Abraham, the promise would be fulfilled when his natural descendant was born; but for Paul, the descendant of Abraham is a spiritual man to whom the races of humankind may be assembled as the House of God, which includes all those God would call to be assembled in this way. Paul's vision, however, far exceeded that of Abraham. God gave Abraham the vision of a race coming from him that would produce the Seed who would fulfill the promise of blessing all nations. But, Paul received a revelation from God, together with the grace of administration, to bring the Gentiles into this promise:

> *Surely you have heard about the administration of God's grace that was given to me for you, that is, the mystery made known to me by revelation….*
> *…This mystery is that through the gospel the Gentiles are heirs together with Israel, members together of one body, and sharers together in the promise in Christ Jesus.*[304]

God always intended that Jesus, the Seed of Abraham, would produce a holy race to be inclusive of all the fallen sons of Adam, irrespective of their human racial origins, since Adam was the first son of God, and all humans ultimately are descendants from him. In the prophetic psalm regarding the role of Jesus as the anointed King over the House of God, David wrote the declaration of God to Jesus: "...You are my son; today I have become your father. Ask me, and I will make the nations your inheritance, the ends of the earth your possession."[305] This, by definition, would be a holy race since they will be returned to God through Jesus, the promised Redeemer of Adam's progeny.

The House of God was to be drawn from all the nations of humankind, and among them the culture of heaven would be on display. Their order would permit the showing of the grace and goodness inherent in the nature of God. Since they would be drawn from the diversity of all the different racial and cultural backgrounds of humanity, the House of God would obviously be a spiritual house.

As Abraham is a natural patriarch to the nation of Israel, the apostle Paul is the spiritual patriarch to the Gentiles. During his lifetime, Paul traveled throughout the Mediterranean bringing the good news to the Gentiles. He was, without dispute, the father to the early Gentile church in the Greco-Roman world.

With the fall of Jerusalem to the Roman armies in August of A.D. 70, Jerusalem was no longer the center of influence of the Christian faith. By then, Paul established the Church in Gentile cities such as Corinth, Ephesus, and Rome, which became the visible order of the New Testament church. This order would remain intact throughout the years of the church's persecution by the Roman authorities until Emperor Constantine changed the model. He reorganized the order of the Church to satisfy the requirements of accountability to a secular empire. This model has prevailed, to the present time, in the form of the state church.

THE CHURCH IN JERUSALEM

The Church started in Jerusalem and was exclusively Jewish and remained that way, until the fall of Jerusalem and the scattering of Israel. Then, the model established by Paul became the preeminent expression of the Body of Christ in the world.

The early Jerusalem model provided insight into how the Body of Christ operated within a city. However, the model established by Paul functioned on all levels, from the basic model of a father and sons to spiritual families, households, regions, and in the lifetime of Paul, arose to become a holy nation among the nations of humankind.

The New Testament presents a picture of the Body of Christ evolving through all these stages to become a complete, though limited, expression of the full intent of God. A part of its evolution is observed within the city of Jerusalem. Among the major developments of that early group of believers was the need for orderly distribution of material resources, because of the oncoming of severe economic problems, and the almost instantaneous unleashing of a virulent persecution against them by the temple authorities.[306] In sharing their common fate, they turned to each other for comfort and help.

The apostles provided leadership and introduced the order of helpers to assist in the orderly and equitable distribution of material aid. They distinguished between an administration that provides spiritual direction and oversight and one that attended to material needs. The apostles devoted themselves to the Word of the Lord and to prayer, while giving instructions that would result in an administration designed to provide an orderly distribution of resources for general needs. They selected seven men to oversee the distribution of resources. They chose these men because they were "full of the [Holy] Spirit and wisdom."[307] The apostles themselves stated, "We will turn this responsibility over to them [the seven] and will give our attention to prayer and the ministry of the word."[308]

The material supply came from the unforced generosity of the early believers themselves. This spontaneous sharing of resources seems to be emblematic of the way they demonstrated their sense of oneness and community. Shortly after the inception of the church on the day of Pentecost, it was noted that:

All the believers were together and had everything in common. They sold property and possessions to give to anyone who had need. Every day they continued to meet together in the temple courts. They broke bread in their homes and ate together with glad and sincere hearts, praising God and enjoying the favor of all the people. And the Lord added to their number daily those who were being saved.[309]

As their numbers grew, the need for order developed. The apostles continued to function in the role of fathers, providing spiritual care and direction to the fledgling church, while the deacons (originally the seven helpers devoted to material supply) were in charge of distributing material aid.[310]

The next great challenge they faced came in the form of persecution. It began with the arrest of the apostles Peter and John following "an outstanding miracle" performed at the very gates of the temple in Jerusalem. The effects of this spectacular occurrence became impossible for the Jewish leaders to ignore. The growing legacy of Jesus of Nazareth had become problematic for these leaders. His influence was spreading rapidly through the teachings of His disciples. These teachings were often accompanied by demonstrations of miraculous power, resulting in a rapid increase in the number of Jesus' followers.[311]

There was a backlash from the temple authorities who became fearful of the growing influence of the disciples of Jesus and the connection that was being made between His crucifixion by the Romans and their collusion with the temple authorities. The face of this persecution was that of a young rabbi, from Tarsus of Cilicia, who was studying in the temple at the time. This young rabbi, whose name was Saul, was the point of contact between the backlash from the temple and the persecution of the followers of Jesus.

Instead of discouraging them, the persecution had the effect of hardening the believers' resolve. With the killing of Stephen, one of the seven deacons, the believers were widely scattered.[312] For a time, only the apostles remained in Jerusalem. After Saul (renamed

Paul) was converted, the persecution seemed to have abated and the Church began to reestablish itself again in Jerusalem. However, a new round of persecution was launched, and it claimed the life of James the brother of John, and Peter himself was imprisoned.[313]

At this point, public meetings in the temple were no longer possible, so they began to gather privately in homes. During this time, some of the apostles and deacons ventured beyond Jerusalem. Peter visited the home of Cornelius, a Roman centurion who was stationed in Caesarea, and the first Gentile converts were added to the Church.[314] Philip went to Samaria and many converts resulted from his visit. Peter and John were later dispatched to help establish the church in that area.

The Jerusalem church at the beginning established a sense of community among the believers, together with an accompanying order that resulted in their spiritual growth, and the proper distribution of material resources. It was sometime later, following the persecution in Jerusalem and the initial scattering of many believers into the Gentile world, that an order emerged that was more encompassing than that which initially emerged in Jerusalem. Paul would lead this advance among the Gentiles, and the order of the Church would take on greater complexity as it met the challenges both within and outside of Jerusalem. Slowly the picture emerged of the Body of Christ comprising both Jews and Gentiles.

Eventually the church in Jerusalem would face extreme economic hardships and would receive material supply from among the Gentiles, establishing the Church as a nation among the nations of humankind. This result was achieved after many hard-fought battles that required enormous changes of mindsets, particularly among the Jewish believers.

The central figure leading this advance was Paul, the young Jewish rabbi formerly named Saul, who initially led the persecution of the Church on behalf of the Jewish authorities. His apostolic administration directed the rapid rise of the Church in the Greco-Roman world and brought the issue of reconciliation between Jews and Gentiles in the Body of Christ to the forefront. Once the matter was finally laid to rest, following an apostolic council in Jerusalem,[315] the Church's growth among the Gentile nations was quite rapid. By the fall of Jerusalem in A.D. 70, there were multiple centers of the Christian faith in places such as Ephesus, Corinth, and Rome itself. The Jewish influence upon the Church ended abruptly with the destruction of Jerusalem, and the order that Paul established became the foundation for the rule of the Church.

PAUL'S ADMINISTRATION OF THE MYSTERY OF THE BODY OF CHRIST

For this reason I, Paul, the prisoner of Christ Jesus for the sake of you Gentiles—

Surely you have heard about the administration of God's grace that was given to me for you, that is, the mystery made known to me by revelation, as I have already written briefly. In reading this, then, you will be able to understand my insight into the mystery of Christ, which was not made known to people in other generations as it has now been revealed by the Spirit to God's holy apostles and prophets. This mystery is that through the gospel the Gentiles are heirs together with Israel, members together of one body, and sharers together in the promise in Christ Jesus.

I became a servant of this gospel by the gift of God's grace given me through the working of his power. Although I am less than the least of all the Lord's people, this grace was given me: to preach to the Gentiles the boundless riches of Christ, and to make plain to everyone the administration of this mystery, which for ages past was kept hidden in God, who created all things. His intent was that now, through the church, the manifold wisdom of God should be made known to the rulers and authorities in the heavenly realms, according to his eternal purpose that he accomplished in Christ Jesus our Lord. ...For this reason I kneel before the Father, from whom every family in heaven and on earth derives its name.[316]

It is clear that Paul himself is the instrument by whom the mystery and its administration are revealed to the rest of the apostles.[317] Paul begins his journey by taking others with him. Barnabas and his cousin John Mark are among his early traveling companions who set out from Antioch.

After Paul and Barnabas separate over the issue of John Mark's reliability, Paul chooses Silas and Timothy to accompany him on his next major journey. Over time, many others become part of the company with whom he travels and works. After some period of time, Paul begins to refer to Timothy as his beloved son. He also refers to entire groups of people as his children, and begins to speak and act as their father.[318] He instructs Timothy to pattern his ministry after his experience in his relationship to Paul: "You then, my son, be strong in the grace that is in Christ Jesus. And the things you have heard me say in the presence of many witnesses entrust to reliable men who will also be qualified to teach others."[319] Paul had found in Timothy a reliable son whom he raised to become a leader in the Body of Christ. His fatherly dedication to Timothy is expressed in this admonition. Paul traveled with Timothy for many years and exposed him to the same kind of discipleship that Jesus extended to His twelve disciples. As with Jesus and the twelve, Paul's relationship to Timothy was that of a devoted father and a faithful son. Just as the twelve became the leaders of the Church in the first generation, the disciples of Paul, such as Timothy and Titus, matured to become the leaders of the second generation and provided the continuity necessary for the advance of the Kingdom in succeeding generations.

Paul considered believers in entire cities to be his spiritual children. As has been noted earlier in his letter to the Corinthians, he addressed them with the familiarity of a father who was displeased with their immaturity, divisiveness, arrogance, and lack of moral conviction. He understood that he had a duty to confront them and to demand that they change their way of life to conform to the standards that he had established both by his instructions and his way of life.

His influence extended beyond individuals and cities to entire regions. He gave orders to the churches of Galatia to set aside sums of money on a regular basis to relieve the brethren in Jerusalem in a time of severe famine.[320] Paul and Barnabas established the church in cities such as Antioch, Iconium, Lystra, and Derbe within the region known as Galatia. The same was true to an even greater extent among the churches in the region of Macedonia,[321] which included cities such as Philippi, Thessalonica, and Berea.

Thus is the unfolding of Paul's administration. He starts out as a spiritual father to sons such as Timothy and Titus. Then his spiritual family grows to include a household in many cities. As his influence extended over regions, those who look to him as a spiritual father exert influence comparable to the clans within the tribes of Israel. His clans are not limited to a single region, but are spread throughout the Greco-Roman world. By the time he appeals to Caesar and is sent to Rome, he is the undisputed leader of the Christian faith outside of Israel. He is the patriarchal figure in the Church among the Gentiles.

Paul used his standing as a father of men to disciple them to maturity so that they could fulfill their destinies. His sons who endured the discipline of their training under his hand became mature leaders who could be trusted to faithfully represent the Lord in cities, regions, and nations. He left Timothy in Macedonia and Titus in Crete to establish the elders in the cities of those regions, so that the people of God could be cared for in the fashion in which the early apostles arranged the order of the House of God in the city of Jerusalem. From this place, as a father of a household within a city, he challenged those of his household to accept fully all believers within that city, whether they belonged to his household or to others, such as the households of Apollos or Peter.[322] He forcefully argued for the unity of the Body of Christ, not only among households but also among entire races.[323]

Where his influence extended to regions, Paul called upon the clans to gather resources and to send aid to the Jews who had largely rejected his apostleship and his influence. Though Paul was undoubtedly the patriarch of the Gentile church, he recognized the influence of the other leaders among both the Jews and Gentiles. He expanded the early governmental form of the apostolic council to include representation from the apostles who worked among the Gentiles,[324] establishing the format for the resolution of matters of significance to the entire Body of Christ.

Paul's administration served to accomplish the equally important goals of disciplining and training individuals to maturity so that they could fulfill their personal destiny, while maintaining the unity of the House of God. In pursuing the latter goal, he was uncompromising in his opposition to sects and denominations, and never failed to speak boldly and consistently in advocating and supporting the one Body of Christ. It was always clear to him that the order in the House of God was meant to display the order that is in heaven, since it is the same house whether it is in heaven or on the earth.

CHAPTER 16

A Holy Nation

The relationship between God and man is the most comprehensive and complex relationship one can experience. The unique aspects of the relationship highlight this fact: God is Spirit while man is spirit clothed in flesh; heaven is the seat of God's government while earth is the dwelling place of man; God loves man and created him for a specific destiny; man has free will and may choose between God's purpose for him and his own way; both God and man have a common enemy who opposes God by alienating man from God; and, God took on the form of man in order to reconcile man to God.

In order to show completely all of the different facets of the relationship, God structured human relationships to act as types and shadows of His relationship to man. Consequently, all the forms of human relationships that God established are veiled portrayals of His relationship to man. The metaphors of human relationships are mysteries revealed fully in their appointed time. Examples of common human relationships that are "profound myster[ies]" are the father and son relationship and the husband and wife relationship.[325] These two relationships in particular are used to show that the exact representation of another is possible only through sameness of being.

A dissimilar being will highlight the differences in beings

through their representation. A servant cannot represent the character of his master because he is unfamiliar with both the character and the position of the master. However, his skill allows him to perform the task assigned to him. A son, by contrast, may represent the character of his father because he originated from within the being of his father. He possesses the requisite sameness of being, and he is his father's heir, so he is seated in his father's position when he represents his father to others. That is why a son may say, "Anyone who has seen me has seen the Father,"[326] and "I and the Father are one."[327] That angels lack the requisite sameness of being is also the reason that angels are incapable of exact representation of God.[328]

A marriage highlights the principle of sameness and exact representation, when viewed from a heavenly perspective. Adam came out of God and so was a son who was capable of representing God, his Father. Eve came out of Adam in the flesh and out of God in the spirit, so she was both the son of Adam and the son of God. She was made to exactly represent both. As a representative of both God and her husband, a wife is entitled to the protection of those sources of authority.

A king and his relationship with his kingdom help reveal the divine intentions regarding authority and representation. Understanding a king as sovereign helps to define the origin and function of authority. Similarly, the structure of a kingdom helps delineate the duties and benefits associated with being under authority. In the case of the Kingdom of God, Christ, the King, is the source of authority defining both the benefits and the duties associated with the Kingdom.

A house, such as the one God established, portrays the divine principle of a continuity of purpose. A house, consisting of a multigenerational family, shows the continued connection of a family to a father's plan. The house itself monitors the progress of the unfolding and fulfillment of that plan over long periods of time. The order of the arrangement of the house is important to maintain continuity of purpose, to which end a family's history may be chronicled through the maintaining of a meticulous genea-logical record. These records serve as a kind of self-proving affidavit, certifying the claims of sons in any generation to the promises arising out of the covenants of their fathers. This order mirrors the same one into which Jesus arrived, in the fullness of time, as the Son of God, to finish the task of redeeming the House of God in accor-dance with the requirements of the most ancient of covenants.

Finally, a nation serves to reveal the mystery of God's character. From the beginning, God designed His House to display the glory of His order to the world. He arranged for the testing of the heav-enly order in an environment of complete human diversity, replete with all of the conflicts inherent among human beings. Because of the extreme complexity of the relationship between God and man, no single metaphor sufficiently can capture all its facets.

Consequently, God has employed a range of relationships de-signed to highlight structural aspects of the complete relationship. These metaphors describe this relationship from its most intimate forms to its broadest corporate expressions—from a father and son to a holy nation. Each relational model carries the substance of the primary relationship, that of father and son, through to the broadest context, one in which an entire nation puts on display the nature of God the Father in relationship to Jesus Christ the Son. The cumulative result is a broad display of the relationship among the nations of the world, but with a depth of integrity that is fo-cused on the most basic functional relationship.

God always intended that His House exist on the earth as a nation among the nations. The order of its government is meant to give humankind insights into the nature of God Himself, since all governments inevitably put on display the nature of their sovereigns. Heaven is unwaveringly committed to the forming of this reality upon the earth.

THE GLORY OF THE LAMB

John the apostle was an old man when he was exiled to Patmos, an island off the coast of Ephesus in the Aegean Sea. This would seem a cruel fate for one who had served God for most of his very long life. But, God brought him there to give him the greatest revelation of Jesus he would have, and with it an insight into heaven's priority that would shape the course of history for all of the remainder of the age of man. It was from there that John, the last of the twelve original disciples, was invited into heaven to witness the formal decrees that would create a holy nation on the earth.

By that time, it had been a generation since the gospel was first preached on the day of Pentecost. Peter and all of the witnesses present on that day were dead. Even Paul by now was dead. Only John was left. The order of Judaism had been dismantled with the destruction of the temple in Jerusalem. John himself had lived for many years in Ephesus, and he was now a very old man. He was the most visible transitional link between the first generation of the early church and the next generation.

Often, God will introduce the new order of things from heaven in one generation and will advance its implementation in the succeeding generation. For example, He delivered the ancient Hebrews from slavery in Egypt in one generation and brought them into the Promised Land in the next. Even a generation that sees the astounding works of God may become like an old wineskin as it relates to the further advancement of the things that were introduced in their day. The first generation of believers grappled with the influence of Judaism and also with the admission of Gentiles into the faith. The gains that were made in that first generation could easily have become the new traditions, though they fell far short of the full intention of heaven.

In order to prepare a generation to receive the complete revelation of what had been released into the earth, God waited until a new generation had arisen with a new mindset. He had also removed the obstacle of Judaism by permitting the destruction of the temple and the associated religious culture. Through John, He installed the next great increment of the unfolding picture in a new generational wineskin.

Jesus appeared to John on the island of Patmos in a vision, in which Jesus was holding seven stars in His right hand as He was walking among seven candlesticks.[329] In the encounter, Jesus revealed the twin mysteries of the seven stars and the seven candlesticks: the seven candlesticks were the believers in seven cities in the Roman province of Asia Minor, today the country of Turkey; and the seven stars were seven messengers to the believers in seven cities. Each messenger was given a distinctive message for the group to which he was sent. The messages were urgent and timely but unique to the existing circumstances and characteristics of the particular city. The messages were about things that were to occur shortly as well as conditions among the believers that were in urgent need of address.[330]

After Jesus had given John the messages, He vanished. John next saw an open door into heaven, and a voice invited him to enter the door into that realm to witness the opening of the seven seals on the scroll in the hand of the Almighty God.[331] When the Lamb, who is "the Lion of the tribe of Judah," was found worthy to open the seals,[332] heaven erupted in a song of praise. This song had never been sung before, not even in heaven:

> *You are worthy to take the scroll and to open its seals, because*
> *you were slain, and with your blood you purchased men for*
> *God from every tribe and language and people and nation.*
> *You have made them to be a kingdom and priests to serve our*
> *God, and they will reign on the earth.*[333]

Heaven honored Jesus the Lamb by declaring that He had accomplished God's will on earth. Following John's witness to these events in the spiritual realm, Christ's accomplishments were released on earth as they were declared and celebrated in heaven.

The future imperative for earth was that heaven would bring forth a holy nation drawn from every ethnicity, gender, and social class. Those comprised within the nation would speak different languages and come from all different cultural backgrounds, yet they would be united under the sovereignty of Christ as a nation of royal priests. As Abraham's nation's purpose was to bring Jesus the man into the world, so this holy nation of royal priests would display all of the characteristics found in the Christ. Each member would present that unique aspect of Christ he was created to display. But the complete revealing of Christ would be through the corporate entity, the holy nation, whose purpose would be

> *...to equip his people for works of service, so that the body of Christ may be built up until we all reach unity in the faith and in the knowledge of the Son of God and become mature, attaining to the whole measure of the fullness of Christ.*
>
> *Then we will no longer be infants, tossed back and forth by the waves, and blown here and there by every wind of teaching and by the cunning and craftiness of people in their deceitful scheming. Instead, speaking the truth in love, we will in all things grow up into him who is the head, that is, Christ. From him the whole body, joined and held together by every supporting ligament, grows and builds itself up in love, as each part does its work.*[334]

The first generation of the early church did not possess the necessary culture to receive the fullness of the revelation of a holy nation comprising people from such diverse origins. By the second generation, however, it was normal to think that believers from all over the known world made up the Body of Christ. This change was necessary in order to accommodate the full accomplishment of Christ on the earth, consistent with the declarations that John was called to witness in heaven. This would be the ultimate fulfillment of the precreation covenant.

THE RELEVANCE OF A HOLY NATION

God sent Jesus into the world to reveal His love for all human beings. He is certain that when humankind understands the true nature of His love, all those who yearn to be reconciled to Him will come home to Him.

From the time of Adam's separation from God, the culture of humankind has continued to degenerate to its present state. All of the forms of order that God designed for man's benefit have been polluted beyond recognition by the continuing effects of the fall. The order of husband and wife has been repositioned from exact representation and rule for the benefit of the one under authority, to mistrust of God's order of authority and even competition between husband and wife. Individual obsession with provision and protection has eviscerated the father and son relationship and has sundered the trans-generational heritage of families. The loss of these relational patterns has resulted in a destruction of these foundations for the defining of purpose and for trans-generational continuity. The only remaining reliable basis upon which people may depend are the legal protections afforded them by the law, procedures, and institutions of the nation in which they hold citizenship.

Even an orphan is a citizen of a nation. The last hope of man for the assurance of provision and protection is in the laws and administration of a nation. This arrangement, however, is subject to the control of the strong and the powerful and is increasingly coming under the influence of the skillful and unscrupulous.

The earth is in desperate need of a model of order and peace in which the problems of humankind are subject to permanent resolution. The solution lies in a nation of people "from every tribe and language and people and nation" that reveals the mystery of God the Father and Jesus Christ the Son by demonstrating the goodness of God. The order of a holy nation has the power to redeem men to God from the furthest depths of their brokenness and fallen estate. This is the promise of a holy nation.

Let Them Be One in Us

Father, the hour has come. Glorify your Son, that your Son may glorify you. For you granted him authority over all people that he might give eternal life to all those you have given him.

191

> *Now this is eternal life: that they know you, the only true*
> *God, and Jesus Christ, whom you have sent. ... [t]hat all of*
> *them may be one, Father, just as you are in me and I am in*
> *you. May they also be in us so that the world may believe that*
> *you have sent me. I have given them the glory that you gave*
> *me, that they may be one as we are one—I in them and you*
> *in me—so that they may be brought to complete unity. Then*
> *the world will know that you sent me and have loved them*
> *even as you have loved me.* "[335]

Jesus prayed to the Father that the believers would all be one in the model of His relationship to the Father, as previously set forth. Jesus' view in making this request was that the people of the world would see that the Father loves them in the same way that He loved Jesus. This ultimate expression of the many as one encapsulates the gospel of the love of the Father.

Jesus asked for a configuration of oneness, modeling the relationship between the Father and the Son, in a corporate form that is visible to the world. Christ intends to present His relationship to the Father through this corporate form to the world, which knows neither the Father nor the Son. His intent is that, through this particular presentation, the world will become acquainted with the nature of the Father's love—not only for Jesus and the corporate body of believers, but for the world. The most complete expression of the gospel of the Father and the Son is reserved for this form.

The world cannot see the spiritual Body of Christ; spiritual things are spiritually discerned.[336] Their vision of the spiritual Body of Christ must be presented in a familiar form in order for them to recognize it and to understand the message that it is configured to convey to them.

Since every human being belongs to a nation, God designed an expression of the Body of Christ to function as a nation among the nations of humankind. As such, the governance of this nation must be clear and distinct so that it is observable to the world, and the quality of life that results from this form of governance bears a direct relationship to the order of this nation. God, therefore, designed a holy nation to receive people from every tribe, language, people, and nation to be arranged under the authority of Christ as "a royal priesthood [and] a holy nation."[337] John was invited into heaven to witness the formality of heaven's declaration of its commitment to present the glory of the Lamb within this form upon the earth.

This holy nation is designed to show how people from all of the divisions within the human community may be reformatted into spiritual families, households, clans, tribes, and ultimately, a nation capable of receiving any person in any condition and developing them to the place of a mature son of God. Humans with the most shattered lives could be rescued and restored to such completeness that they are available to put on display the very nature of God in the form they were created to exhibit.

This restorative process is rooted in a relationship to a human father who replicates the role of God the Father in a person's life. The spiritual father is central to the order that rescues a person and restores his destiny. A person saved in this way is placed within the context of a holy nation that empowers and enables him to put on display all that God designed him to be.

The display of the love of God within this context is both pristine and reliable, since all relationships are ordained by God and acknowledged by the participants. These voluntary relationships connect people into a corporate form that does not rely on natural human associations such as race, ethnicity, and socio-economic compatibilities for its strength and power. Within this nation, it would not be unusual for the father and son relationship to defy the prevailing social order. It would be commonplace, for example, for an Arab to be the father of a Jewish person, and a Jewish person to be the father of a Persian. It would not be unusual for an Indian to be the father of an Afrikaner, and a White person to be the father of a Black person, or vice versa. Spiritual families comprise diversities that would be unimaginable in conventional society.

Fathers enable sons to fulfill their destinies by preparing the way for them and by giving inheritances of every kind to enable their progression toward mature representation of God. This holy nation is free of both xenophobia and the spirit of genocide, both of which are scourges that put on display the basest nature of human beings. Husbands love wives as they love themselves in the model of Christ and the Church; and wives replace competition with husbands with exact representation, which presents a picture of oneness that starkly contrasts with the present order of domestic relations. All those in authority rule for the benefit of those under their authority, showing the picture of God's rule, and those under authority recognize the benefit to them of obeying that authority so that they might enjoy an environment of peace, while they grow to their own complete maturity.

A nation that puts on display the love of the father for his son in its forms of order and government will stand in absolute contrast to all other nations.

A City Upon a Hill

Now it shall come to pass in the latter days
That the mountain of the LORD's house
Shall be established on the top of the mountains,
And shall be exalted above the hills;
And peoples shall flow to it.
Many nations shall come and say,
"Come, and let us go up to the mountain of the LORD,
To the house of the God of Jacob;
He will teach us His ways,
And we shall walk in His paths."
For out of Zion the law shall go forth,
And the word of the LORD from Jerusalem.
He shall judge between many peoples,
And rebuke strong nations afar off;
They shall beat their swords into plowshares,
And their spears into pruning hooks;

Nation shall not lift up sword against nation,
Neither shall they learn war anymore.
But everyone shall sit under his vine and under his fig tree,
And no one shall make them afraid;
For the mouth of the LORD of hosts has spoken.
For all people walk each in the name of his god,
But we will walk in the name of the LORD our God
Forever and ever.
"In that day," says the LORD,
"I will assemble the lame,
I will gather the outcast
And those whom I have afflicted;
I will make the lame a remnant,
And the outcast a strong nation;
So the LORD will reign over them in Mount Zion
From now on, even forever.[338]

Although the popular emphasis of the gospel has long reflected a focus of escaping the present evil age by going to heaven, Jesus spoke of a gospel that put on display the nature of the Father. Jesus referred to this prophecy and instructed His disciples that they were "the light of the world" and "[a] city that is set on an hill [that] cannot be hid."[339] God always intended to culminate the age of man with this expression of the gospel in the world. Jesus Himself came to show us the Father and prayed that all those who would believe in Him would live corporately in the model of how He and the Father lived. The prophecies regarding the order of the Church at the end of the age never speak of an urgent escape in the face of growing opposition. Instead, they present a picture of a people whose lives are characterized by righteousness, peace, and joy in an age of depravity, lawlessness, and chaos.

The House of God stands as a holy nation before the nations of the world, while the cycles of war, violence, and injustice decimate the hope of humankind and keep the peoples of the earth deeply divided. Within the House of God, the nations will have come to such harmony and peace that they will have "beat[en] their swords into plowshares and their spears into pruning hooks."[340]

The economy of the House of God will not in any way be dedicated to the enterprises of war and conflict. While among the nations of the world there will be the continuing cycle of "wars and rumors of wars,"[341] in the House of God, those same nations that are at war with each other in the world will live together as fathers and sons.

Whereas current religious thought wistfully hopes for peace and makes pronouncements to that end, there remains no model for the instruction of the nations in how to transition to that result. Peace remains elusive, and looming conflicts all but cause the hearts of men to despair. Because religion fails to see the model of a holy nation, although it has been repeatedly presented in the Scriptures as the ultimate offering of God to man, foreseeing the complete expression of the love of God, religious division continues to be a major contributing factor to human hopelessness.

The prophecies regarding the elevation of the status of the House of God to that of a city on a hill envision that when the corporate Christ is so lifted up, the nations will be drawn to Him for answers. Whereas, the religious Church has historically positioned itself to co-opt the culture of nations and to infiltrate its politics as a way of creating a favorable climate for the receiving of its message, the strategy of God presented through a holy nation is that of a distinct alternative, separate and apart in its identity and governance. It is this clear alternative that God intends to use in the last days to present the message of the Father and the Son as the complete expression of the love of God.

The House of God is this holy nation that God envisioned when He brought Adam into the world. The rule of righteousness is the order of the House of God. God originally gave Adam dominion over the earth to introduce this way of heaven within the natural creation. Jesus came to recapture this mandate and to give it complete expression as the template upon which His corporate Body would function. God intended that the corporate Body of

Christ, functioning globally as a holy nation among the nations of humankind, would express this message completely. God swore to Himself before the worlds were formed to bring the age of man to a conclusion by displaying Himself in the earth in the glory of this form.

> *The seventh angel sounded his trumpet, and there were loud voices in heaven, which said: "The kingdom of the world has become the kingdom of our Lord and of his Messiah, and he will reign for ever and ever." And the twenty-four elders, who were seated on their thrones before God, fell on their faces and worshiped God, saying: "We give thanks to you, Lord God Almighty, the One who is and who was, because you have taken your great power and have begun to reign.*[342]

> *But the court will sit, and his power will be taken away and completely destroyed forever. Then the sovereignty, power and greatness of all the kingdoms under heaven will be handed over to the holy people of the Most High. His kingdom will be an everlasting kingdom, and all rulers will worship and obey him.*
>
> *This is the end of the matter....*[343]

nd Notes

1. John 14:18.

2. See Revelation 13:8 NKJV.

3. Matthew 4:4; Luke 4:4. See John 1:1 NKJV, "In the beginning was the Word, and the Word was with God, and the Word was God."

4. Ephesians 3:14-15.

5. Kaisa Raatikainen, Nonna Heiskanen, Seppo Heinonen, "Marriage Still Protects Pregnancy." BJOG: an International Journal of Obstetrics and Gynecology, Vol. 112, pp. 1411-16 (Oct. 2005).

6. Kathleen Kiernan, "Childbearing Outside Marriage in Western Europe," Population Trends, Vol. 98, pp. 11-20 (1999 Winter); see Kaisa Raatikainen, Nonna Heiskanen, Seppo Heinonen, "Marriage Still Protects Pregnancy," BJOG: an International Journal of Obstetrics and Gynecology, Vol. 112, pp. 1411-16 (Oct. 2005). Birth statistics: Births and patterns of family building England and Wales. Office for National Statistics, FM1 No. 36–2007 (Dec. 15, 2008).

7. Center for Disease Control and Prevention. "Cohabitation, Marriage, Divorce, and Remarriage in the United States," Series Report 23, Number 22. 103, pp. (PHS) 98-1998 (July 2002); http://www.cdc.gov/nchs/data/series/sr_23/sr23_022.pdf (accessed Mar. 17, 2011). See Center for Disease Control and Prevention. "Marriage and Cohabitation in the United States: A Statistical Portrait Based on Cycle 6 (2002) of the National Survey of Family Growth," Series 23, Number 28, p. 8 (Feb. 2010), showing decreased probability for survival of first marriage among white women in comparison to 2002 report. Available at http://www.cdc.gov/nchs/data/series/sr_23/sr23_028.pdf (accessed Mar. 17, 2011).

8. UN. 1994. "Rape and abuse of women in the areas of armed conflict in the former Yugoslavia." General Assembly A/RES/48/143 (Dec. 25, 1993). Available at http://www.un.org/documents/ga/res/48/a48r143.htm (accessed Sept. 21, 2009); R. Charli Carpenter, "Born of war: protecting children of sexual violence survivors in conflict zones" (Kumarian Press, Inc. 2007). Available at http://books.google.com/books?id=PxTEvHSR_vUC&lpg=PA21&ots=HtPpkPVCnA&dq=former%20yugoslavia%20victimization%20children&pg=PA21#v=onepage&q&f=false (accessed Nov. 23, 2010).

9. Matthew 19:8 KJV.

10. Ibid.

11. Genesis 1:26-27: "Then God said, 'Let us make man in our image, in our likeness, and let them rule over the fish of the sea and the birds of the air, over the livestock, over all the earth, and over all the creatures that move along the ground.' So God created man in his own image, in the image of God he created him; male and female he created them."

12. Luke 3:23-38: "Now Jesus himself was about thirty years old when he began his ministry. He was the son, so it was thought, of Joseph, the son of Heli...the son of Enosh, the son of Seth, the son of Adam, the son of God."

13. Genesis 1:11: "Then God said, 'Let the land produce vegetation: seed-bearing plants and trees on the land that bear fruit with seed in it, according to their various kinds.' And it was so."

14. Genesis 1:24: "And God said, 'Let the land produce living creatures according to their kinds: livestock, creatures that move along the ground, and wild animals, each according to its kind.' And it was so."

15. Genesis 1:29-30: "Then God said, 'I give you every seed-bearing plant on the face of the whole earth and every tree that has fruit with seed in it. They will be yours for food. And to all the beasts of the earth and all the birds of the air and all the creatures that move on the ground—everything that has the breath of life in it—I give every green plant for food.' And it was so."

16. Genesis 1:26, see note 12.

17. Genesis 1:27.

18. Hebrews 12:9. Hebrews 12:7-11: "Endure hardship as discipline; God is treating you as sons. For what son is not disciplined by his father? If you are not disciplined (and everyone undergoes discipline), then you are illegitimate children and not true sons. Moreover, we have all had human fathers who disciplined us and we respected them for it. How much more should we submit to the Father of our spirits and live! Our fathers disciplined us for a little while as they thought best; but God disciplines us for our good,

that we may share in his holiness. No discipline seems pleasant at the time, but painful. Later on, however, it produces a harvest of righteousness and peace for those who have been trained by it."

19. It is no distinction of man's that his body was formed out of the earth. Genesis 1:9: "And God said, 'Let the water under the sky be gathered to one place, and let dry ground appear.' And it was so." Genesis 1:11: "Then God said, 'Let the land produce vegetation: seed-bearing plants and trees on the land that bear fruit with seed in it, according to their various kinds.' And it was so."

20. Hebrews 9:27-28: "Just as man is destined to die once, and after that to face judgment, so Christ was sacrificed once to take away the sins of many people; and he will appear a second time, not to bear sin, but to bring salvation to those who are waiting for him."

21. 1 Corinthians 15:42-44: "So will it be with the resurrection of the dead. The body that is sown is perishable, it is raised imperishable; it is sown in dishonor, it is raised in glory; it is sown in weakness, it is raised in power; it is sown a natural body, it is raised a spiritual body. If there is a natural body, there is also a spiritual body."

22. Galatians 3:26-29: "You are all sons of God through faith in Christ Jesus, for all of you who were baptized into Christ have clothed yourselves with Christ. There is neither Jew nor Greek, slave nor free, male nor female, for you are all one in Christ Jesus. If you belong to Christ, then you are Abraham's seed, and heirs according to the promise."

23. It was the Spirit of God itself that is said to have made man a "living being." Genesis 2:7: "the LORD God formed the man from the dust of the ground and breathed into his nostrils the breath of life, and the man became a living being."

24. Hebrews 1:5: "For to which of the angels did God ever say, 'You are my Son; today I have become your Father'? Or again, 'I will be his Father, and he will be my Son'?"

25. Romans 8:16-17 KJV: "The Spirit itself beareth witness with our spirit, that we are the children of God: And if children, then heirs; heirs of God, and joint-heirs with Christ; if so be that we suffer with him, that we may be also glorified together."

26. Genesis 5:1-2.

27. Terug naar Friedrich Weinreb, Translations: Adam and Adamah. Available at http://www.geocities.ws/fweinreb_documentation/Tradam.html (accessed June 16, 2011):

Linguistically the word Adam, "man", is often related to the word "earth", viz. adamah. It is said (as linguists often conclude superficially) that Adam was so called because he had been taken from the earth. Yet this is essentially completely wrong, also linguistically. Indeed, the word "man", Adam, comes from the word "I resemble", so resemblance. This means to say that man was made in the likeness of God. The word "likeness" has the same stem as "man"; so the essential of man is not that he was taken from the earth but that he resembles God, like God said at Creation that He would create man to his image and likeness. Accordingly the word "adamah", earth, comes from "man". It is the feminine form of "man", and the woman is always younger than the man, comes after the man, and through man the earth is indeed deified, brought to God. It is not so that the earth forms man, but man must form the earth.

It is typical to see that this linguistic error is made in times of materialism, when the feminine side of man, this earthly life, is emphasized. But in times when it is known that man is also divine, that indeed the divine in man is the determining factor, it never occurred to people to say that Adam comes from adamah, because it was very well known that the feminine was derived from the male, and that the man does not have to conform to the woman.

28. Genesis 1:11-24.

29. Genesis 1:26.

30. Genesis 1:14.

31. An example of which was the appearance of the star as a sign visible in the heaves to men on earth, announcing the birth of the son who would redeem humankind to the purposes of God.

32. Genesis 1:28: "God blessed them and said to them, 'Be fruitful and increase in number; fill the earth and subdue it. Rule over the fish of the sea and the birds of the air and over every living creature that moves on the ground.'"

33. 2 Peter 1:4 NKJV: "by which have been given to us exceedingly great and precious promises, that through these you may be partakers of the divine nature, having escaped the corruption that is in the world through lust."

34. Hebrews 1:14: "Are not all angels ministering spirits sent to serve those who will inherit salvation?"

35. Ephesians 3:14-15.

36. John Milton, hymn, "On the Morning of Christ's Nativity Christmas."

37. Genesis 1:28; see note 33.

38. Matthew 6:10.

39. Luke 2:14 KJV: "Glory to God in the highest, and on earth peace, good will toward men." NIV: "Glory to God in the highest, and on earth peace to men on whom his favor rests."

40. Isaiah 9:6: "For to us a child is born, to us a son is given, and the government will be on his shoulders. And he will be called Wonderful Counselor, Mighty God, Everlasting Father, Prince of Peace."

41. Romans 1:20.

42. Genesis 2:23.

43. See Ecclesiastes 12:7.

44. See John 3:5.

45. See Ephesians 5:22-33.

46. 1 Corinthians 6:17 KJV.

47. Romans 8:16.

48. Genesis 3:12.

49. Genesis 2:17.

50. 1 John 4:7-12.

51. Revelation 21:6.

52. Hebrews 2:10.

53. Hebrews 1:5-6: "For to which of the angels did God ever say, 'You are my Son; today I have become your Father'? Or again, 'I will be his Father, and he will be my Son'? And again, when God brings his firstborn into the world, he says, 'Let all God's angels worship him.'"

    Hebrews 1:14: "Are not all angels ministering spirits sent to serve those who will inherit salvation?"

54. See, e.g., Isaiah 6:1-3: "In the year that King Uzziah died, I saw the Lord, seated on a throne, high and exalted; and the train of his robe filled the temple. Above him were seraphs, each with six wings: With two wings they covered their faces, with two they covered their feet, and with two they were flying. And they were calling to one another: 'Holy, holy, holy is the LORD Almighty; the whole earth is full of his glory.'"

55. Colossians 3:4.

56. Hebrews 3:3-6.

57. 2 Corinthians 5:20-21.

58. Romans 6:23: "For the wages of sin is death, but the gift of God is eternal life in Christ Jesus our Lord."

59. John 10:10 KJV: "I am come that they might have life, and that they might have it more abundantly."

60. 1 Thessalonians 5:23: "May God himself, the God of peace, sanctify you through and through. May your whole spirit, soul and body be kept blame-

less at the coming of our Lord Jesus Christ.'"

61. Genesis 3:5: "For God knows that when you eat from it your eyes will be opened, and you will be like God, knowing good and evil."

62. Romans 8:20-21 NIV (2010): "For the creation was subjected to frustration, not by its own choice, but by the will of the one who subjected it, in hope that the creation itself will be liberated from its bondage to decay and brought into the freedom and glory of the children of God."

63. See Romans 8:22.

64. See Romans 5:20.

65. Genesis 3:8.

66. See Genesis 3:6.

67. 2 Corinthians 5:1-4: "Now we know that if the earthly tent we live in is destroyed, we have a building from God, an eternal house in heaven, not built by human hands. Meanwhile we groan, longing to be clothed with our heavenly dwelling, because when we are clothed, we will not be found naked. For while we are in this tent, we groan and are burdened, because we do not wish to be unclothed but to be clothed with our heavenly dwelling, so that what is mortal may be swallowed up by life."

68. 2 Corinthians 5:19: "that God was reconciling the world to himself in Christ, not counting men's sins against them. And he has committed to us the message of reconciliation."

69. Genesis 1:26.

70. Genesis 2:7 KJV (NIV "living being").

71. Romans 1:20.

72. Philippians 2:12.

73. Mark 14:34; Mark 14:38 KJV.

74. Revelation 13:8 KJV.

75. John 12:27-28 NIV (2010).

76. 1 Corinthians 2:11-14.

77. James 3:15 KJV. Also 1 John 2:15-16 KJV: "Do not love the world or anything in the world. If anyone loves the world, the love of the Father is not in him. For everything in the world—the cravings of sinful man, the lust of his eyes and the boasting of what he has and does—comes not from the Father but from the world."

78. See Genesis 3:10.

79. See John 3:7-8.

80. Philippians 2:5 KJV: "Let this mind be in you, which was also in Christ Jesus." Romans 12:2 NIV (2010): "Do not conform to the pattern of this world, but be transformed by the renewing of your mind. Then you will be able to test and approve what God's will is—his good, pleasing and perfect will."

81. See, e.g., 1 Corinthians 12:1.

82. 1 John 4:18: "There is no fear in love. But perfect love drives out fear, because fear has to do with punishment. The one who fears is not made perfect in love."

83. Romans 2:4 NIV (2010): "Or do you show contempt for the riches of his kindness, forbearance and patience, not realizing that God's kindness is intended to lead you to repentance?"

84. Ephesians 6:11-12.

85. See Hebrews 2:14-15 NIV (2010): "Since the children have flesh and blood, he too shared in their humanity so that by his death he might break the power of him who holds the power of death—that is, the devil—and free those who all their lives were held in slavery by their fear of death."

86. 2 Corinthians 4:4.

87. James Strong, The New Strong's Exhaustive Concordance of the Bible (Nashville, TN: Thomas Nelson Publishers, 1990), G2889. Kosmos, kos'-mos'; prob. from the base of 2865; orderly arrangement, i.e. decoration; by impl. the world (in a wide or narrow sense, include. its inhab., lig. Or fig. [mor.]): -adorning, world.

88. John 3:16.

89. 1 John 2:15.

90. 1 John 2:15-17.

91. Strong, The New Strong's, G2888.

92. John further described these systems, saying, "the whole world is under the control of the evil one," (1 John 5:19); and Paul writes in the letter to the Ephesians that we struggle not against flesh and blood but against the "powers of this dark world," the "kosmokrator" (Eph. 6:12). See also First John 5:4-5 ("[F]or everyone born of God overcomes the world. This is the victory that has overcome the world, even our faith. Who is it that overcomes the world? Only he who believes that Jesus is the Son of God"; First Peter 2:9: "But you are a chosen people, a royal priesthood, a holy nation, a people belonging to God, that you may declare the praises of him who called you out of darkness into his wonderful light."

93. Matthew 4:8-9.

94. Colossians 1:13: "For he has rescued us from the dominion of darkness and brought us into the kingdom of the Son he loves."

95. Matthew 18:15-17.

96. Deuteronomy 19:15.

97. Strong, The New Strong's, G3144. Compare with Strong's H5707, the Hebrew word translated "witness" in Deuteronomy 19:15, which has the singular translation of a spectator or recorder who gives testimony.

98. See Ephesians 3:9-12.

99. Ibid.

100. Hebrews 6:16-20.

101. Revelation 13:8 NIV (2010): "All inhabitants of the earth will worship the beast—all whose names have not been written in the Lamb's book of life, the Lamb who was slain from the creation of the world."

102. God's choice to appear as Father and Son, when He is by nature spirit, is not a limitation on the ability of God to appear in infinite permutations of Spirit, since God, as Spirit, is present in His completeness in each human being who is a son of God. Romans 8:14-16 NIV (2010): "For those who are led by the Spirit of God are the children of God. The Spirit you received does not make you slaves, so that you live in fear again; rather, the Spirit you received brought about your adoption to sonship. And by him we cry, 'Abba, Father.' The Spirit himself testifies with our spirit that we are God's children." God as Spirit is present as His complete self in hundreds of millions of people alive at the same time in the earth, while He is simultaneously seated on the throne in heaven as both the Father and the Son. Acts 7:55-56: "But Stephen, full of the Holy Spirit, looked up to heaven and saw the glory of God, and Jesus standing at the right hand of God. 'Look,' he said, 'I see heaven open and the Son of Man standing at the right hand of God.'" See also Revelation 4.

103. Hebrews 6:13.

104. 1 John 3:8 NIV (2010): "The one who does what is sinful is of the devil, because the devil has been sinning from the beginning. The reason the Son of God appeared was to destroy the devil's work."

105. Genesis 4:3.

106. John 1:29.

107. Matthew 24:35; Mark 13:31; Luke 21:33.

108. Psalm 138:2 NIV (2010).

109. John 1:1-3.

110. Romans 1:21.

111. John 8:12: "When Jesus spoke again to the people, he said, 'I am the light of the world. Whoever follows me will never walk in darkness, but will have the light of life.'" John 9:5: "While I am in the world, I am the light of the world."

112. Matthew 26:39.

113. Hebrews 7:22.

114. Revelation 5:9-12 NIV (2010).

115. John 17:20-22.

116. Colossians 1:12-14 NIV (2010).

117. See Colossians 1:6-8 NIV (2010): "…In the same way, the gospel is bearing fruit and growing throughout the whole world—just as it has been doing among you since the day you heard it and truly understood God's grace. You learned it from Epaphras, our dear fellow servant, who is a faithful minister of Christ on our behalf, and who also told us of your love in the Spirit."

118. Galatians 4:1.

119. John 1:12 KJV.

120. Strong's G5043, "teknon."

121. Romans 8:14; see Strong's G5207, "huios."

122. John 16:7,12-15 NIV (2010).

123. Matthew 12:30 NIV (2010): "Whoever is not with me is against me, and whoever does not gather with me scatters." See Acts 7:51 NIV (2010): "You stiff-necked people! Your hearts and ears are still uncircumcised. You are just like your ancestors: You always resist the Holy Spirit!".

124. Galatians 3:15-18 NIV (2010).

125. Galatians 3:26-29 NIV (2010).

126. 1 Corinthians 15:45-49 NIV (2010).

127. John 3:6-7.

128. Romans 12:2 NIV (2010); Romans 8:5-17.

129. 1 Corinthians 12:12-13,27 NIV (2010).

130. Ephesians 1:3-10 NIV (2010).

131. Ephesians 1:11-14 NIV (2010).

132. Acts 2:31-36.

133. Romans 8:1-2.

134. 2 Corinthians 1:22, 5:5; Ephesians 1:14.

135. Romans 8:6 KJV.

136. John 5:18 NIV (2010).

137. John 5:19-20 NIV (2010).

138. Deuteronomy 5:4-5 NIV (2010).

139. Romans 1:20 NIV (2010).

140. 1 Corinthians 13:12 NIV (2010): "For now we see only a reflection as in a mirror; then we shall see face to face. Now I know in part; then I shall know fully, even as I am fully known."

141. John 6:35.

142. 1 Corinthians 2:14; see also Romans 8:7: "[T]he sinful mind is hostile to God. It does not submit to God's law, nor can it do so."

143. Romans 8:5.

144. Hebrews 11:1 KJV.

145. John 1:1-2,11.

146. 1 Corinthians 2:7-8.

147. 1 Corinthians 2:10 NEB; C.H. Dodd, ed., The New English Bible. New Testament. Oxford and Cambridge: Oxford University Press and Cambridge University Press, 1961.

148. Ephesians 1: 9-12 NIV (2010).

149. Genesis 1:2 NIV (2010).

150. Ibid.

151. Ibid.

152. Genesis 1:9-10.

153. John 1:14 NIV (2010).

154. 2 Corinthians 5:17 NIV (2010).

155. 2 Corinthians 5:16.

156. Galatians 4:19: "My dear children, for whom I am again in the pains of childbirth until Christ is formed in you." Colossians 3:4: "When Christ, who is your life, appears, then you also will appear with him in glory." Romans 8:11: "And if the Spirit of him who raised Jesus from the dead is living in you, he who raised Christ from the dead will also give life to your mortal bodies through his Spirit, who lives in you."

157. 2 Corinthians 4:3-6 NIV (2010).

158. See Hebrews 10:1 and Colossians 2:17.

159. 2 Corinthians 3:7-11 NIV (2010).

160. See Genesis 22:17.

161. Hebrews 8:5 NIV (2010).

162. Hebrews 9:8.

163. 1 Corinthians 14:33 KJV.

164. A man on the highest council of priests in ancient Rome.

165. Ephesians 1:9-10 NIV (2010).

166. Romans 14:17 NIV (2010).

167. 1 Corinthians 15:44-49 NIV (2010).

168. 1 John 3:8.

169. Strong's supra G932. Basileia, bas-il-i'-ah; from 935 [basileus; prob. From 939 (through the notion of a foundation of power; a soverign]; prop. Royalty, i.e. (abstr.) rule, or (concr.) a realm (lit. or fig.): -kingdom, + reign.

170. Genesis 49:8-12 NIV (2010).

171. Genesis 49:3.

172. See Genesis 42:37.

173. See Genesis 43:8-9.

174. See Strong's supra H6557. Perets, peh'-rets; the same as 6556; Perets, the name of two Isr.:-Perez, Pharez

175. See Strong's supra H6556. Perets, peh'-rets; from 6555; a break (lit. or fig.):-breach, breaking forth (in), X forth, gap.

176. Romans 15:4 NIV (2010); see John 5:39-40 NIV (2010) ("You study the Scriptures diligently because you think that in them you have eternal life. These are the very Scriptures that testify about me, yet you refuse to come to me to have life.").

177. Luke 3:38.

178. This is evident from the fact that after this event, God changed the name of Abram to Abraham. Abram meaning "exalted father"; whereas Abraham means "Father of many nations," a title more suitable to the description of God.

179. See Isaiah 11:2.

180. Hebrews 1:3.

181. Colossians 3:3-4.

182. Exodus 33:18.

183. Exodus 33:19-22.

184. Exodus 34:5-8.

185. See Deuteronomy 5:5.

186. See John 1:14.

187. John 14:10.

188. John 1:14 NKJV.

189. John 17:1.

190. Romans 12:1 NIV (2010).

191. John 1:14 NKJV.

192. John 11:40.

193. John 5:22-23.

194. Romans 12:2 NIV (2010).

195. John 5:20.

196. Philippians 2:5-11 NIV (2010).

197. John 17:21.

198. Colossians 1:15,19-20.

199. 2 Corinthians 5:19-21 NIV (2010).

200. See John 1:1-14.

201. Mark 1:1,10-11.

202. See Genesis 3:17-19.

203. Herod had a history of inordinate violence before Jesus was born. He had previously murdered his second wife Mariamne and his sons, Alexander and Aristobulus. It was also widely rumored that Herod had issued a standing order that all the seventy elders of Israel be executed upon his death, so that there would be mourning in Israel.

204. Matthew 2:15. "When they had gone, an angel of the Lord appeared to Joseph in a dream. 'Get up,' he said, 'take the child and his mother and escape to Egypt. Stay there until I tell you, for Herod is going to search for the child to kill him.' So he got up, took the child and his mother during the night and left for Egypt, where he stayed until the death of Herod. And so was fulfilled what the Lord had said through the prophet: 'Out of Egypt I called my son'" (Matt. 2:13-15).

205. Luke 2:49 KJV.

206. Luke 2:52.

207. Hebrews 5:8.

208. The context for the quote from Hebrews 5:8 reads, "During the days of Jesus' life on earth, he offered up prayers and petitions with fervent cries and tears to the one who could save him from death, and he was heard because of his reverent submission. Son though he was, he learned obedience from what he suffered and, once made perfect, he became the source of eternal salvation for all who obey him and was designated by God to be high priest in the order of Melchizedek" (Heb. 5:7-10 NIV (2010)).

209. See Matthew 4:1.

210. Matthew 3:17.

211. John 17:6-12 (showing Jesus' acknowledgement of the disciples, including Judas, as those who God gave to him and of the necessity that one of them would betray him).

212. John 6:70-71.

213. John 17:20-26 NIV (2010).

214. Philippians 2:13 KJV.

215. Luke 22:42.

216. John 10:18.

217. John 15:13.

218. John 10:30.

219. Hebrews 1:1-2 NIV (2010).

220. 2 Corinthians 5:19 NIV (2010).

221. See John 5:19.

222. Matthew 27:46; Mark 15:34.

223. Ephesians 3:14-15 NIV (2010): "For this reason I kneel before the Father, from whom every family in heaven and on earth derives its name."

224. See Romans 8:29 NIV (2010).

225. Malachi 4:5-6 KJV.

226. Matthew 11:14.

227. Luke 1:16-17.

228. 2 Kings 2:9-14.

229. See 1 Samuel 16:1-13.

230. See 1 Samuel 13:14; Acts 13:22.

231. John 1:23 NIV (2010).

232. John 1:29-34.

233. See Hebrews 13:17 KJV.

234. See Hebrews 11:13: "All these people were still living by faith when they died. They did not receive the things promised; they only saw them and welcomed them from a distance, admitting that they were foreigners and strangers on earth."

235. Isaiah 9:6.

236. See Strong's supra H1 "ab." (showing nine separate meanings of the word for "father" as used in the Old Testament including "the head or founder of a household, group, family, or clan"); Id. at G3962, "pater" (identifying the root word for patriarch as having several different meanings, including that of a near or remote progenitor of a family or people).

237. Matthew 23:9.

238. 1 Corinthians 4:14-17 NIV (2010).

239. 1 Corinthians 4:18-21 NIV (2010).

240. See Philippians 2:22; 1 Timothy 1:2,18; 2 Timothy 1:2, 2:1.

241. See Titus 1:4; Philemon 1:9-11.

242. Titus 1:4-5 NIV (2010).

243. Philemon 1:9-12 NIV (2010).

244. See 1 Peter 5:13.

245. See 1 John 2, 5:21.

246. John 3:16.

247. 1 John 2:15.

248. John 3:6: "Flesh gives birth to flesh, but the Spirit gives birth to spirit."

249. Romans 8:11-16 NIV (2010).

250. Hebrews 12:9.

251. 2 Corinthians 11:2.

252. Galatians 4:19-20.

253. John 17:6, 26; see also John 17:9-12: "…I am not praying for the world, but for those you have given me, for they are yours… None has been lost except the one doomed to destruction so that Scripture would be fulfilled…."

254. "Keep constantly obeying your rulers, and constantly be submitting to them; for they themselves are constantly keeping watch over your souls, knowing that they are to give account, that they may do this with joy, not

with lamentation, for this would be profitless to you" (Heb. 13:17 Wuest Exp. Trans.).

255. Note for study: this is the story of the prodigal son.

256. Matthew 28:18-20: "…All authority in heaven and on earth has been given to me. Therefore go and make disciples of all nations, baptizing them in the name of the Father and of the Son and of the Holy Spirit, and teaching them to obey everything I have commanded you. And surely I am with you always, to the very end of the age."

257. Hebrews 1:8-9 NIV (2010): "[A]bout the Son he says, 'Your throne, O God, will last for ever and ever; a scepter of justice will be the scepter of your kingdom. You have loved righteousness and hated wickedness; therefore God, your God, has set you above your companions by anointing you with the oil of joy.'"

258. See Acts 2.

259. Acts 2:17.

260. Romans 8:14 NIV (2010).

261. 1 Corinthians 2:9-10.

262. Colossians 3:1-4.

263. See 2 Corinthians 5:18-21.

264. See Matthew 6:10: "your kingdom come, your will be done, on earth as it is in heaven."

265. Ephesians 3:14-15: "For this reason I kneel before the Father, from whom every family in heaven and on earth derives its name."

266. Hebrews 8:5-6 NIV (2010).

267. Hebrews 8:13 NIV (2010).

268. Hebrews 9:8-11 NIV (2010).

269. Hebrews 9:23-24 NIV (2010).

270. See Genesis 31:30.

271. See Genesis 24:1-9.

272. See Joshua 6:24.

273. See Joshua 7:1-6.

274. See Joshua 7:10-12.

275. Joshua 7:14-15 NIV (2010).

276. Joshua 7:1 NIV (2010).

277. Joshua 7:16-18 NIV (2010).

278. See Joshua 7:20-21.

279. Joshua 7:25-26.

280. Joshua 7:24.

281. Strong's supra H1004. Bayith, bah'-yith; prob. From 1129 abbrev.; a house (in the greatest var. of applications, espec. family, etc.).

282. See Genesis 14:14.

283. Genesis 18:17-19.

284. Deuteronomy 6:1-9.

285. Deuteronomy 11:18-21 NIV (2010).

286. Exodus 13:14-16.

287. Genesis 12:1-4 NIV (2010).

288. Leviticus 25:10-25 NIV (2010).

289. Genesis 15:18-21 NIV (2010).

290. See Joshua 13:14.

291. See, e.g., 1 Chronicles 23,27 showing David's organization of the Levites and the listing of the heads of households of each tribe.

292. See, e.g., Ezra 8; Nehemiah 7, 11 (listing exiles by families and showing provincial organization by families and tribes).

293. Romans 5:16-17 NIV (2010): "Nor can the gift of God be compared with the result of one man's sin: The judgment followed one sin and brought condemnation, but the gift followed many trespasses and brought justification. For if, by the trespass of the one man, death reigned through that one man, how much more will those who receive God's abundant provision of grace and of the gift of righteousness reign in life through the one man, Jesus Christ!"

294. Exodus 19:5-6.

295. Deuteronomy 5:5: "At that time I stood between the Lord and you to declare to you the word of the LORD, because you were afraid of the fire and did not go up the mountain."

296. See Exodus 19:22, 24 referencing "priests" among the people, even though this is before the creation of the Levitical priesthood and the people are still in the state of coming out of Egypt. Before God established the order of Levi there was an existing order of priests among the people, the order of Melchizedek.

297. See Genesis 14:18-20; see Hebrews 7.

298. Romans 11:13-23 NIV ("kindness"); see also KJV ("severity").

299. 1 Peter 2:4-10.

300. Hebrews 10:1.

301. Romans 1:20 NIV (2010): "For since the creation of the world God's invisible qualities—his eternal power and divine nature—have been clearly seen, being understood from what has been made, so that people are without excuse."

302. Ephesians 2:11-22.

303. 1 Corinthians 4:14-21 NIV (2010).

304. Ephesians 3:2-6.

305. Psalm 2:7-8 NIV (2010).

306. See Acts 4–8.

307. Acts 6:3.

308. Acts 6:3-4. The term "deacon" was applied to this function, as it is descriptive of the activities of an attendant or waiter who runs errands and performs aid service, usually of a menial sort. Such a person typically has a gift of helps and takes pleasure in serving others.

309. Acts 2:44-47 NIV (2010).

310. Note for study: This fulfilled Jesus' prophetic symbol given to the Jews on the occasions when He fed multitudes of five and four thousand respectively: "'…Do you still not see or understand?'" Jesus asked His disciples, "'Are your hearts hardened? Do you have eyes but fail to see, and ears but fail to hear? And don't you remember? When I broke the loaves for the five thousand, how many basketfuls of pieces did you pick up?' 'Twelve,' they replied. 'And when I broke the seven loaves for the four thousand, how many basketfuls of pieces did you pick up?' They answered, 'Seven.' He said to them, 'do you still not understand?'" (Mark 8:17-21). Jesus Himself was the Bread from heaven, and would supply the need for spiritual and natural food of His followers. The first distribution of this supply occurred when the twelve apostles undertook the spiritual care of the Jerusalem church while delegating the task of distributing material goods to the seven deacons.

311. See Acts 3:11 to 4:21.

312. See Acts 7 and 8.

313. See Acts 12.

314. See Acts 10.

315. See Acts 15.

316. Ephesians 3:1-15 NIV (2010).

317. See Galatians 2:6-10.

318. See, e.g., 1 Corinthians 4:14-21.

319. 2 Timothy 2:1-2.

320. See 1 Corinthians 16:1-4.

321. See 2 Corinthians 8:1-15.

322. See 1 Corinthians 1:10-13.

323. See Galatians 3:26 and Ephesians 2:19-22.

324. See Acts 15.

325. Romans 16:25-27 (discussing the father-son relationship as a mystery): "Now to him who is able to establish you in accordance with my gospel, the message I proclaim about Jesus Christ, in keeping with the revelation of the mystery hidden for long ages past, but now revealed and made known through the prophetic writings by the command of the eternal God, so that all the Gentiles might come to faith and obedience—to the only wise God be glory forever through Jesus Christ! Amen" (NIV 2010). See Ephesians 5:31-32 (discussing the husband-wife relationship as a "profound mystery"): "'For this reason a man will leave his father and mother and be united to his wife, and the two will become one flesh.' This is a profound mystery—but I am talking about Christ and the church" (NIV 2010).

326. John 14:9. Jesus' continuing discussion in this section further evidences the sameness of being He has with the Father: "…Anyone who has seen me has seen the Father. How can you say, 'Show us the Father'? Don't you believe that I am in the Father, and that the Father is in me? The words I say to you I do not speak on my own authority. Rather, it is the Father, living in me, who is doing his work. Believe me when I say that I am in the Father and the Father is in me; or at least believe on the evidence of the works themselves. Very truly I tell you, all who have faith in me will do the works I have been doing, and they will do even greater things than these, because I am going to the Father. And I will do whatever you ask in my name, so that the Father may be glorified in the Son. You may ask me for anything in my name, and I will do it" (John 14:9-14 NIV 2010).

327. John 10:30.

328. Hebrews 1:5.

329. See Revelation 1:9-19.

330. See Revelation 2–3

331. Revelation 4:1.

332. Revelation 5:5.

333. Revelation 5:9-10.

334. Ephesians 4:12-16 NIV (2010).

335. John 17:1-3, 21-23 NIV (2010).

336. 1 Corinthians 2:14 (NIV 2010): "The person without the Spirit does not accept the things that come from the Spirit of God but considers them foolishness, and cannot understand them because they are discerned only through the Spirit."

337. 1 Peter 2:9.

338. Micah 4:1-7 NKJV; also Isaiah 2:2 NIV (2010): "In the last days the mountain of the LORD's temple will be established as the highest of the mountains; it will be exalted above the hills, and all nations will stream to it."

339. Matthew 5:14 KJV.

340. Isaiah 2:4; Micah 4:3.

341. Matthew 24:6; Mark 13:7.

342. Revelation 11:15-17 NIV (2010).

343. Daniel 7:26-28 NIV (2010).

SoleynPublishing LLC

www.soleynpublishing.com

contact@soleynpublishing.com

PO Box 67456, Albuquerque
NM 87193-7456, USA

 facebook.com/soleynpublishing

 twitter: twitter.com/SoleynPublish

Generation Culture Transformation
Specializing in publishing for generation culture change

Visit us Online at:
www.egenco.com
www.egenbooks.com

Write to: eGen Co. LLC
824 Tallow Hill Road
Chambersburg, PA 17202 USA
Phone: 717-461-3436
Email: info@egenco.com

 facebook.com/egenbooks

 twitter.com/vishaljets

 youtube.com/egenpub

 egenco.com/blog